My Voice in Power
The Story

Nyasher Browne

spread your wings, speak your truth, write it down & let it iii
go

This book is not about trying to shame any one as I am grateful for every positive contribution that everyone who I have written and anyone who has ever been in my life has given me.

All names of the people involved have been changed

I would like to say a special thank you to my friends in Maidenhead for helping me in my time of need especially those who were able to come forward and speak to the police.

I would also like to say a special thank you to my friends in Reading who also helped me in my time of need and to those who still support me now and have been a great shoulder of strength whilst I put this book together.

The biggest thanks go to my children and my brother

CONTENTS

MY VOICE IN POWER

I can't believe it, that I'm finally here I never thought that I would make it this far. Let alone even be alive on some days but on Saturday the 14th of November 2020 I'm officially happy to say that I am. Many people say that 40 is when life begins, but I believe that life begins everyday with the different choices you make but being 40 is when you may see it start to see it come together and are more accepting of your journey. This does depend on who you are and what you've been through. Some people may or may not make these realisations at all, some do it younger and some may do it older.

So here I am two weeks, well thirteen days to be precise before my 40th birthday making more realisations and accepting and embracing ones I've made before, ready to get more things done and tell you my story so far.

CHAPTER 1

Now that I have a clearer mind, I can remember that as a child I had always wanted to be a ballerina, ice skater, nurse, or midwife. As I got older an air stewardess and author had found their way onto the list. I'm surprised being an author wasn't there first although I was more of a reader than a writer. I had been taught to read from a noticeably early age using a variety of sources including the newspaper.

I grew up in a house with my grandmother a small framed fair skinned lady with a slight number of freckles on her face, with ever-changing hair styles of braids and curly perm. With a laugh so deep that I'm sure could be heard for miles around. She wrote as she talked and was always full of advice, now married to her second husband was of dark skin with a level head of hair and a distinctive moustache and no beard with a deep voice which sounded deeper whenever he sang. He came over via invitation from a friend who was already settled as a result of the Windrush and worked in an abattoir before working in Mars, where worked until he left the country. My nan had come over from the Caribbean in the sixties I think, she had many jobs including working on the market, the Gillette factory, and what was known as the Ramada Hotel. She still had children at home when she took me in her, second daughter and four stepchildren from her husband, a daughter and three sons.

We lived in a three bedroomed house with my nan and her husband having the biggest room which had a door with lock on that you needed a key for. I had to share the room the next size down with my step aunty and aunt, not only did we share a room we also had to share a double bed. Can't say it was too bad though as my aunt was out most of the time. It was my step uncles that I felt for having to share a box room and a bunk bed. My step uncles all looking like they could pass as triplets with the same skin tone features and haircut, but there were a few years in between them. I don't like to call them step aunt and uncles as I grew up with them like they were my brothers and sisters.

My step aunty was very petite and slim with shoulder length curly permed hair that she always wore down. Later wearing it in the same way but with a relaxer instead. She studied pharmaceuticals and had a passion for football and when she was being affected by her Sickle Cell, she loved to play it. My aunt was also short but very well developed in the chest area. People often said they could see er breasts coming before they could see her. Braids and beads were her favourite style always with a fringe, but this changed as she aged.

They all went to school and college, and I enjoyed playing out in the garden wearing my aunt's turquoise stilettos and her hot pink ones, she had red ones too. I always made sure I put them back in wardrobe before she got back though so I didn't get in trouble for wearing them. My step aunty didn't have things like that she was more of a collectable's person. I remember she had a pink piggy bath set with string tissue paper for the bath water with these tiny silky bath bombs in it. I took one out once and popped it and then wiped it all over the wardrobe door. I have no idea why, but I do remember getting into trouble for that. My favourite thing in our room aside from my toys was this old style coloured paper with the word BREAK drawn on it in graffiti writing, made to look three dimensional with pencil shading.

For my toys I had many teddies my favourite's being a Glo Worm and Roland Rat teddy. I also had a pink dolly bath with blue taps for my Barbie dolls and an orange bath for my Sindy dolls and a few My Little Ponies. Being the youngest in the house I played by myself quite a lot so having a good imagination was extremely helpful. I had cousins that used to visit but I stopped sharing my toys with them when one day my cousin, who was a lot taller than me with dual heritage skin and curly hair cut the hair on one of my dolls and broke its foot.

As my aunts and uncles were of age, they would be the ones who took responsibility for me when my nan and her husband, who I called dad weren't home. But to be fair apart from when I was a baby, I don't think I took much looing after I was usually quite good at keeping myself entertained, prancing and dancing around and singing songs. They ensured I got to and from nursery safely, although one morning I had quite a fall. The slope leading down to the nursery was covered in gravel. Not sure if I was running or just slipped but either way, I went flying down the slope with knee dragging along the gravel. I remember the nursery teacher taking the gravel out of knee and cleaning up the cut and putting a plaster on it. I cried for quite a while as to be fair it was quite deep in fact so deep it has left a scar. All my aunts and uncles took it in turns to take me to nursery, but I remember going mostly with my step aunty and a few times with my youngest step uncle, well up until he died.

That happened when I was five and I think he was about seventeen or eighteen. He had suffered for quite some time, probably from since childhood I imagine due to how severe his Sickle Cell was.

Sickle Cell is a disease is a condition that affects the red blood cells, there is also Sickle Cell Anemia which is a more serious type of the condition. It is common in the African and Caribbean background and is usually inherited.

The disease causes bodies to produce unusually shaped red blood cells which do not live as long as healthy blood cells and they can also block blood vessels. This has serious and lifelong implications, but treatment can help to manage some of the conditions. The main symptoms of this disease are painful episodes which are called sickle cell crisis. They are very severe and can last up to a week affecting the hands or feet, ribs and breastbone, spine, pelvis, tummy, arms, and legs. The number of times a crisis happens varies from person to person. The risk of infections is increased and due to the red blood cells being misshaped they struggle to carry oxygen around the body which can cause tiredness and shortness of breath. Having this can also increase the risk of strokes and some people have problems with their lungs and can suffer with gallstones.

Nearly everyone who suffers with Sickle Cell has Anemia but not everyone inherits full Sickle Cell some people only have the trait of it as both parents may not have Sickle Cell.

The above information is what I have shared with you from my knowledge for a more detailed explanation and proper medical knowledge you should talk to a medical professional or organization.

I remember my youngest step uncle always laying up on the sofa when he was home and as time went on if he wasn't on the sofa, he was in hospital. I knew he was ill but obviously at the time too young to understand the finer details. Sometimes I would go away for weekends, and he wouldn't be there when I came back. Apart from this one time, I came back with a white paper bag full of mix up sweets. I remember having one in there that looked like a tablet and thinking that would help him I gave it to him, saying "here you go Uncle this will make you feel better." He ate it and I'm not sure if was moments later or just on the same day he began vomiting to the point where it was like he just couldn't stop and that was it he was back in hospital again and never came out. When I realised, he hadn't come back out of the hospital I felt I was to blame for giving him the sweet, like the tablet had killed him. But it wasn't meant to do that it was meant to make him better.

I don't really have any recollection of the funeral but for some reason I remember wearing a red velvet dress with a white lace thrill round the front of the neck, white pulled up knee length socks and red shiny shoes. I feel like that was the day of the funeral.

My step aunty had sickle cell too, but I don't ever remember her being sick until after this, it was like she suddenly had crisis after crisis screaming and crying in the night and screaming out "I don't wanna die" and she would vomit a lot too. Most of the time her condition was managed at home, I think...as I don't really remember her going into hospital as much as my youngest step uncle did. But her painful nights were very intense especially when she had gallstones.

I felt incredibly sad her for but there was nothing I could do except lay with her and be sure not to give her any sweets so she didn't die, although on really bad nights I would sleep with my nan and her husband. I remember one time it happened; it was the night before the younger years of the school were told to take the day off. Due to how bad the night had been I was kept off that day too. When I went in the day after I was mocked by the class as they thought I had got the information wrong and had just decided to take the day off. I just sat and rocked on my chair until they had finished.

It was a while before she had a crisis again especially like that one and she went back to studying at college, working, and going to uni. One of my favourite achievements of my step aunty was when we went to go and watch her do a recital where she played the keyboard and sang 'gimmie hope Joanna.'

By this time if my memory has served me correctly my aunt had moved out by then as she had got pregnant, and we clearly didn't have room for a baby in the house. She first revealed to me that she was pregnant when she was about six or eight months. She had been hiding it by wearing baggy jumpers and leggings. When she told me, we were sat on the side wall in the front garden and she let me feel the baby move, it was so weird yet so intriguing at the same time. She must have either revealed herself or got found out at this point because she then had a place of her own. When she had the baby, I was allowed to visit and did so quite often and me and my little cousin built up quite a bond.

CHAPTER 2

No one really came to our house on a regular basis, so it was usually a special occasion, the first big occasion I recall is my fifth birthday. I had a big party and was allowed to invite everyone from my class. The living room although quite big was full, we had a Transformers video for the boys and Care Bears for the girls, however I liked them both as much. We had toys out played games and had plenty of food, including a pink birthday cake with colourful candles. Other than that, our house was only busy over Christmas and New Year. I used to love Christmas so much, we got woken up early in the morning and got dressed up to the smell of freshly baked bread and the dinner cooking. The dinner table would be fully extended with places set, fresh bread on the table and slices of freshly baked ham and piccalilli to go on top. I'm sure there were other items, but these are the ones I can remember. Ooh we also had pots of tea and half a grapefruit in a bowl with sugar sprinkled on top, which we had to eat first. After breakfast we would pull a cracker and then help clear up and reset the table for later. When we would have more food consisting of all the usual Christmas food traditions, followed by a song and dance from me and the Queens speech. People used to come and say hi and some would eat. At the time I didn't really know who they were but the atmosphere in the house used to change, and Christmas was the only time I ever saw those people. As inquisitive as I was, I didn't ask any questions.

I'm sure I must have seen her many times before, but a lady used to come and see me and for a while she had strong features and a nervous but strong laugh and always made a funny noise with her throat, she took me to my Ballet and tap dance classes. I soon learnt that she was my mum. I think I knew that before, but I can't really register being told. It kicking in didn't happen 'til much later. I enjoyed Ballet, wearing a blue leotard, and learning all the little moves. I did Tap dance as well which I also enjoyed but didn't get to do much of.

It was around the age of eight I believe that it really registered that my mum was my mum. Growing up with my nan and her husband, having their own and stepchildren living with them obviously the words mum and dad were used a lot. I think I was told that my nan was my nan and not my mum but that never really stuck until around the same time even though I still called my nan mum after being told.

I was going up to bed one night and whilst I stood on the bottom step of our brown carpeted flight of stairs, wearing my white quilted dressing gown with red flowers on and a pair of old tights on my head. I said, "goodnight mum." Both my nan and my mum were sat together at the dining table, which lived at the back of the living room. My mum looked up at me and said goodnight. But this wasn't the response I was expecting well rather it was not who I was expecting the response from, so I said it again, "goodnight mum." My actual mum replied again, this went on for a little while, surprisingly. Until someone said, "well how many more times you gonna say goodnight?" it took a moment but that's when I realized I needed to say goodnight nanny instead and when I did that's when my nan replied. From that day onwards I realized the importance for their wellbeing rather than mine that I needed make sure that I called my nan, nan when my mum was around. A bit confusing considering, I called my nans husband dad but then mind you he was never around my dad in the same room long enough for the same mistake to be made. I believe that this is because by the time my dad was allowed to see me things were already awkward and pleasantries from him were the bare minimum expected after beating up my mum whilst in a relationship with her and getting her pregnant with me when she was sixteen and he was twenty-one. Then just to top that he off slept with someone and got engaged to her leaving my mum to find out via the local newspaper. So, his visits were literally hi and bye as he was picking up and dropping off. He was a short guy of a muscular build; he still had his Bajan accent and being a Rasta, he was very particular with the food he ate only having fish, veg, rice, pasta, potatoes, fruit, eggs, and gold top milk. If these requirements couldn't be met, then he wouldn't eat or drink and preferred not to from others if he could help it. His locks weren't as long as he wanted them to be, but he did his best to maintain them until he cut them off many years later. Being proud of his locks at the time he even locksed up his beard. His eyes were very deterring as though he had two sets, like an eye behind the eye like he had two different stories to tell from two different souls.

I never discussed my situation with anyone, but I knew my situation was different and was made more difficult by the fact that my mum would visit with a baby sometimes who was my brother. He was red skinned being of Jamaican descent with a vivid imagination. In his early adulthood he was often described as looking like the music artist Ludacris. As he got older, he would come round, and we would spend time together and play the usual games of hide and seek and the floor is lava. And get into the usual kind of trouble for running around the house and climbing on the furniture. We calmed ourselves down one day though after knocking over our nans porcelain fruit bowl that had a layer of red apples, a layer of lemons and another fruit on the top. Lucky for us it was a clean break, so we were able to place it on the top and just avoid it other than getting up to turn over the tv.

When I was old enough or when someone would take me, I would go and visit my mum and my brother at their flat where they lived. By then I had another sibling it all seemed a bit weird, and this point I started to wonder why I didn't live with them. It was so weird going to the same school but going home to different houses but leaving via different school entrances meant that it wasn't on my mind every day.

Like some children being brought up by separate parents I used to see my dad on weekends but only occasionally as there were other people who were quite present in my life and so would spend a lot of time with them. Patrick and Sylvia, they were called. They had a good friend called Peter a dark-skinned kindhearted Rasta man with long locks, well that's how I remember him to be who was also friends with my mum he even had a thing with her at one point, which I only found out about recently after asking questions from looking back at pictures.

Patrick was a short white man who wore glasses and never wore anything other than shirt and trousers with dress shoes, when going out he would wear the jacket to match. His wife Sylvia also white and the same height as him with brown curly shoulder length hair, she sounded like someone from a sitcom when she spoke and always gave more of a giggle than a laugh.

One-night Peter wanted to go out and my mum wanted to go but didn't have a babysitter, so Peter asked his friends Patrick and Sylvia. They were due to go on holiday the next day but agreed with my mum and Peter on the understanding that if they were not back to pick me up on time they would still go on holiday and so would leave me on the doorstep. Thinking about it now, I'm not sure if I ever asked if they made it back on time or if they just collected me from the doorstep.

Either way they got back from their holiday and I'm here telling the tale and staying with Patrick and Sylvia at weekends and then that increased to being during school holidays.

They took me and my brother on many adventures, we went on seaside trips and often went to see the lights in Blackpool and London. One of my most memorable trips to London was when my brother lost his balloon. We got one each and they had tied mine to my wrist so it wouldn't blow away and get lost. However, my brother was not feeling

this and insisted on just holding the balloon. He was warned that if it got lost, he wouldn't get another. Things were going well until that very thing happened. As we were walking along; we could hear the start of a whimper and looked round to see the balloon floating away from my brother as he began to break into a cry. Patrick did his best to try and catch the balloon, he even climbed some of a tree but to no avail. This made my brother even more upset and the fact that he couldn't get another one made him worse. He screamed and cried for hours, not even sweets distracted him. Sweets were one of the main reasons we loved going to London because we knew were allowed to get giant colourful lollipops. my brother still got his and Patrick tried his best to reason with him, but Nev was having none of it. As soon as Patrick's back was turned Nev went charging behind him and smacked him on the bum with his Lolly which then cracked into small pieces. Don't quite remember how the day ended but I'm fairly sure my brother must have slept well last night.

Back then we were allowed to sit in the airports and eat in the restaurants even when you weren't going anywhere and sitting at the airport watching the planes was one of my favourite things to do as well as going to the Beefeater restaurant and actually watching the Beefeaters outside of Buckingham palace. One time though Patrick and Sylvia did take me away on holiday, I was about four and they took me to Holland where we stayed for about a week, I think. We stayed in a small hotel which was owned by a guy named Mr. Pillar who I took immense pleasure in calling Mr. Caterpillar, I don't remember what he looks like, but I took magnificent pleasure in seeing him every morning to order and be served my boiled egg and soldiers. And once I had finished, I would turn the eggshells upside down and pretend that I hadn't eaten the eggs. I very vaguely remember the tulip fields and windmills. I enjoyed a trip to the model village, and I definitely remember having a tantrum over wanting a pair of clogs. I Had a lovely picture taken there too which I still have.

On our regular weekends we often spent time at one of Patrick's sisters' houses which was rather and large and she had a great garden but me and my brother loved going there for strawberries dipped in sugar but sadly she passed away.

Even though I never fully understood the concept my first encounter of being made aware of skin colour causing a problem was when I was in town walking through the Butts Centre holding onto Patrick with one hand and my Gollywog in the other, that Sylvia had spent time collecting coupons for from the Marmalade jars. We saw a Police Officer who proceeded to chase after us and question Patrick. Wanting to know who he was and what he was doing with me and where we were going. Then stating that he had to ask with their being a difference in skin colour. We were then left to go where we were going so, we continued towards Patrick's home going my favourite way so we could go up the spiral concrete stairs.

They lived somewhere different before this place I only remember staying there a few times and not liking it as the mattress felt like it had bugs crawling inside it when I slept. This new place was much better even though they only had one room it was big enough for their double bed and bedroom furniture and a fold up bed for when I stayed. The kitchen was a perfect square with a little hatchet which I loved getting my food passed through as the dining table was placed underneath it on the other side in the living room. Porridge in the morning and roasts in the evening or steak and kidney pie and chips. With chips being freshly peeled and chopped with a chip cutter and then fried. Everything was all perfectly set up and had my own cup and saucer and special finger placement cutlery so I could use a knife and fork properly.

As my brother and sister got older, they also came and spent time with me at Patrick and Sylvias but that soon got put a stop to when my youngest sister on my mums' side misbehaved whilst we were there and had a tantrum so bad, she bit Patrick. And boy did she get punished for that, in fact that was the first time I see her in so much trouble. Despite her consequences, we were never allowed to go there again, but we did stay in touch.

I was so gutted as that's where I had the best toys, I loved my colourful saucepans with faces on and the plastic wooden spoon to match, my black baby with the magic flow milk and orange juice bottles, which I ended up drawing on in green felt tip one day when I was angry. I had a specially made wicker stool that was green and brown I used that to sit on whilst I listened to my story tape Disney books when every time you hear the chime it's time to turn the page.

Even into adulthood I stayed in touch with Patrick and Sylvia and went to see them whenever I could, and they got to meet my children too. Not long after having my youngest Patrick got testicular cancer and had an aneurism. At this point Patrick and Sylvia had moved again into supported housing so they could receive help. In the end the Cancer began to eat away at Patrick and so he had to continue his last days in hospital. The first time I went to visit him at the hospital it was like he was not really there but was, if that makes any sense. As he was highly medicated with morphine but in between random moments he was talking like he was making sense even if at times he was only making sense to himself. But he rose up and looked at me and said "it's you. Well, that's it everything makes sense now." He laid back down and then had to get up again because he started to choke. I froze in panic and nurse came over to see to him, reassured me and then back to see to others.

The second time I went with my brother, Patrick was in a side room by then, but it didn't feel right as the room was packed with close family and friends to not seem rude, we stayed a little rather than walking out as soon as arriving. The last time I went to visit him was the last time I went and had to go. I got there and it was just Sylvia and Patrick's sister. In a way it was like he was almost waiting for me to get there before he went. Sylvia was near the foot of his bed and Patrick's sister was near his head on the same side as Sylvia. So, I took off my coat and went round the other side and took his hand and touched his head and it was at that moment he let go. His head tipped to the side as if he were seeking more comfort from my hand and then black liquid trickled from his mouth. I heard a voice say that's the cancer he's gone now. That was his sister, and the room went quite until his sister then said it was like he was waiting for you. I looked up to see she was talking to me.

My brother came with me to say a final goodbye in the chapel of rest Patrick was dressed smartly with some medals on, not sure what they were for. He never really talked about his life I just knew he was around in the war and didn't like to talk about it other than that the most I knew was that he worked in a carpet shop, married Sylvia and didn't have children. Seeing Patrick for the last time in the chapel of rest didn't seem to be as bad as we thought it would be, we thought it was odd to feel that way but then just put it down to us knowing he was of a

certain age. We felt sorry for Sylvia as we knew she heavily relied on

Patrick and didn't have any family of her own to support her in anyway. Me and my Partner at the time did what we could to help when we could and when my relationship with broke down, I still continued to help her when I could and in between those times Sylvia had carers and paid helpers. It was challenging work but I'm glad I helped when I could as Sylvia soon died herself. I did what I could to help with funeral arrangements and sorting through her things and that's where a lot of my childhood photos are from. I picked blue clothes for her funeral outfit because that was the same colour outfit she buried Patrick in and now they are together again.

CHAPTER 3

On the weekends that I wasn't with Patrick, and Sylvia I was with my dad. The only memory I have of him from when I was younger was him taking to me to stay at my sister's house. Where me and my sister put up her dolly's cots and tried to see if we could sleep in them. Before we did this though our dad came in to say goodnight and we asked him about what he was smoking, which was a spliff. He let us try some, not to sure how we were at smoking given that we were so young. I think about 3 or 4. my sister is a year older than me, and my mum found out my dad being with her mum when she announced their engagement in the local newspaper. I'm not sure what happened but the place where I went to see my dad on the weekends had changed. He was staying in a room with another woman who soon after had a baby. This was my second brother. During this period, I didn't see much of my older sister and never stayed at her house again. My dad moved from this room into a flat where he went on to have two little girls. I started to see more of my dad at this time and then my older sister started to come and stay as well but she didn't like his girlfriend who I thought was nice. I think my sister felt that the woman was the reason our dad wasn't with her mum anymore. I don't ever remember us doing much we just played with our siblings and sat around until Sunday evenings when it was time to go home again.

I didn't know much about my dad then, but he soon did something that made me, and my sister question him. One weekend whilst we were staying, we could hear what we thought was a conversation. Soon after we heard a noise and we started to consult with each other about what the noise was. We decided that it sounded like a slap. We put our heads together to come up with a story to go back in the living room saying that we were going in there for sweets that were in a bowl in the living room, so we could see if he had hit her. When we went in her had her face covered with her hand and tears in her eyes but tried her best not to let us see. There was nothing we could do and nothing like that was seen or heard again until I was 14.

As I mentioned earlier, I lived with my nan and her second husband, back then I didn't know my nans first husband who was obviously my grandad, he was from St. Vincent like my nan and had an afro like Don King but bigger and had what we called the Browne nose, as everyone from his line of descent had the same shape nose. I later learnt that the relationship between him and nan was abusive and that's why it hadn't lasted and that's why I didn't know who my grandad was at that age.

It wasn't until my mum moved to Maidenhead that we got to meet him and know who he was because of him threatening to sue her or something because he didn't get to see us. At this time there was something on the news about grandparents taking their children to court for not being able to see their grandchildren, so I guess this is where he got the idea from.

We never stayed there alone we always went as either me and my brother or me, my brother and sister. We never really got on with his wife but obviously as children there wasn't much, we could do, so we just did as we were told.

On our first visit we sat in the garden and talked to him whilst he smoked a cigar and kept an eye on what the gardeners were doing. We stayed again after the wedding of him and his second wife, which I don't actually remember going to, but we were given a slice of cake which we had to cut again to share between the three of us. The funniest thing that happened whilst we were there was my brother falling off the bed and splitting his pyjama trousers. Our worst moment was when my grandad had struggled to get up the stairs to make it to the toilet on time and wet himself on the way. He struggled because he had had most of one of his legs amputated instead of his wife helping him, she laughed and made fun of him whilst we stood uncomfortably and looked on not knowing what to say or do. We never went back after that and didn't see him again until he was in hospital before he died.

I was out playing at the time when my mum got the call the weather was dingy and grey and for some reason, I had a fight with a girl at the top of the park. My mum wasn't best pleased when I got back not because she knew I was fighting but because she had been looking for me as she wanted to head to the hospital. We all went to see him but when we got there his wife wouldn't let us in and then argument broke out and we left.

As we drove back home with my mum in the passenger side and me, my brother sister in the back and my mums second oldest stepbrother Levi was driving. My nan had, had two children in St. Vincent before coming to England. I just welled up and tears just filled my eyes and streamed down my face. Didn't even know why I was crying to be honest. My mum asked what was wrong and I didn't have any answers and my mum's second oldest brother told her to just leave me.

The next few weeks after was really weird as I had never seen my mum this way before, my mum seemed heavy, and the atmosphere was grey. My mum was struggling to stomach food and the morning of the funeral she made cups of coffee and bacon sandwiches for all the adults in the house, but it made my mum heave, and she couldn't even stomach the smell let alone the taste. After the funeral, the heaviness continued for a day or so more and then it seemed like that was it. That chapter was over just like the closure of a book.

Although we did have a little green armchair that he had given us when used own a taxi rank and I still have it now, but it could do with reupholstering.

Even though I was the youngest in the house I wasn't really bullied like in a typical sibling household so that was great for me and having grandparents for parents meant I had more luxury treatment. Shopping was fantastic I got to go on every trip and was always allowed to have a trolley for myself, so I was in charge of choosing most of the snacks. At that time Kwik save was the place to go, with a choice of plastic bags. Either 1p or 3p bags with the 3p ones being thicker and stronger than the 1p ones. The thick ones were always great at being reused by my step uncles to practice their head spins when they were practicing break dancing in the living room.

Every week we would always get the variety cereal packets and my nan would leave one out for me in a bowl every morning before she left for work. If it was a toast morning, she would leave out the little jam packets that she got from working at was then known as the Ramada hotel.

The added bonus was that my nans husband who we will call Isiah was working at Mars, so we were never without sweets and other than anyone else who had relatives that worked at Mars were always the first to try new sweets when they came out. I almost found a downside to that one day, that was when Skittles came out. I saw them in the bag when Isiah came home the night before, but it was too late for me to eat sweets. So, I knew I had to be up first to get them in the morning. The sweets were kept in their bags hung up above the freezer in the cubby hole opposite the kitchen, so being careful not to make too much noise going through the beads that were hung in the living room doorway. I got the sweets and took them with me to school, stopping in the shop along the way to get my all-time favourite, a Kit Kat. I had hold of the sweets but had to put them down to get my change organised so I could pay. The shop keeper was looking at me over the counter with an unsure look on his face until he decided to ask what I had in my hand and as he was about to say I needed to pay for them he made the realisation that they were something he didn't sell but was still curious as to where they came from so, I had to explain about Isiah working at Mars. Even though I liked the attention it got me at school, having sweets that no one had seen before I decided it was best not to do the same thing when the Dove ice cream bars came out.

spread your wings, speak your truth, write it down & let it   27
go

When I wasn't stuffing my face or wearing my aunts heals out in the garden, I would play with our dog Rex, he was small with a black silky-smooth coat. He went missing one day and was kept by some people who lived across the road and down the hill from our house. We don't know how he got out but one morning when my nan was going to work to, she saw the people with the dog. She called him but they wouldn't let him come to her, she was so angry, but I guess there wasn't much that could be done about it as I don't think we had any proof.

I only ever remember my nan and Isiah arguing once, but it was quite bad well it sounded it anyway I never heard what was being said but I do remember raised voices and smashing glass and slamming doors. I was upstairs being looked after by my aunts and uncles and still to this day I have idea what it was about. But other than that, times were good we used to go to events down at Central Club there was always a dance or family event being held down there. One of which I won, it was a fancy-dress competition, and I had my body wrapped up in a patterned material and then had a different one wrapped around my head and was called an African Queen. My reward was a trophy and a trip to Whipsnade Zoo. Unfortunately, these things don't happen there now and there are a lot of talks surrounding the community club about whether it should be knocked down. The reasons against being the mural that was painted on the side and how long it has been there. Even for me as an adult it was the place to go as it was the best Caribbean food spot in town, it was also used as a youth club, a social club, and a place where people could go and use PCs. Everyone's favourite part was the kitchen which was called Perry's, well known for its rice and peas, curried meats, and ground food soup. Followed by well-known Caribbean drinks such as Guinness punch, peanut punch, fruit punch and sea moss. Perry's is still going strong but has had to relocate due to the closure of the building by our local council.

CHAPTER 4

My aunt had moved out and had her own place which was about thirty minutes away in a three bedroomed house. I think she just had a room at first though because when I used to go and stay there, I remember we had to share a bed with her. She had, had her baby by this time and he slept in his cot. He was of dual heritage and his skin looked whiter than he did mixed or black, but he definitely had black features as he had the Browne nose.

The only reason I remember this is because she had a man stay over and he shared the bed with us too and one night in particular, she was obviously in the mood and encouraged him to have sex with her. I heard him say that they couldn't because I was in the bed, and she responded by saying that it was okay because I was sleeping. I wasn't I was just lying there quietly but at that point it was clear it was best for me not to speak. Then it began a whole heap of moving around and heavy breathing getting deeper the longer they went on for. I had no idea what they were doing at the time but obviously I do now.

The other rooms must have vacated after a while as her place became the spot where everyone chilled. They would eat food, play music, drink, and take drugs. She even had police officers that would pop in during the day whilst on their lunch or in passing and then come back later in the night the join the gathering. One of the girls that used to come there ended up being my aunt's longtime friend. She used to love eating bean straight from the tin. I always sat next to her as she always talked to me. We continued to be in touch for many years after her and my aunt stopped being friends. They fell out over money as my aunt ripped her off. We don't talk now either as her drug habit ended up getting the better of her. But she remembers, when I was eight me asking her what she was putting in a Rizla paper, she said she told me it was mint. But I told her it wasn't and that it was weed, and I knew because that's what my dad smoked. I also stopped having to share a bed with her after that and as my cousin grew, he had his own room where I would also sleep when I stayed. They got freaked out one night though as my cousin had started sleepwalking, they were a bit concerned at one point in case he had taking something as he stood in the living room with his eyes wide open and not responding, but then started playing with his toys. My aunt knowing that waking him up especially suddenly could cause him to have a heart attack gently talked, him back up the stairs. It was a nice house the only thing I didn't like about it was the green bathroom that always had slugs in it at some point. My only rule whilst I was at my aunts was to help with my cousin and not to use the teaspoons that they had used to put white powder in their coffee that they had left on the kitchen side. In the third room was the youngest of my mum's brothers Tony. He had permed hair and a moustache and of a muscular build with a gap between his two front teeth which is another we all have. He seemed to laugh a lot, but people didn't find him funny a lot of the time especially when he couldn't keep his hands to himself. he always had the same look of the flat Mohican, because of his curls and wore jeans and vests. He seemed like he was a to the point guy and like he didn't care what anyone else thought. I say that because I remember when my brother used to get really bad nose bleeds in the summer. And it happened one day when we were coming back from the shop, a clot was coming out of my brothers nose and this uncle just stopped in the street and pulled it and pulled it until it all came out, not caring who was watching. He also didn't care when people were moody towards him when he was annoying them.

One week when I stayed there the fair was in town, I went with my aunt and her friends and filled up on and sweets, candy floss, coke, and chips. Going on every ride available in between finishing off with my favourite, the cage. On the way home I took a bit of a funny turn and spent the night throwing up black sick. After feeling sorry for myself for a few days and feeling like things couldn't get any worse, I started to feel better and just lay awake reading to my baby cousin who wasn't that much of a baby anymore but still very young 'til he fell asleep. I seemed to spend more time with than I did my own siblings. I lay awake just looking up at the ceiling until Tony came in and asked if I was okay. I said yeah and he then asked if I was bored and I was, so I said yeah. He asked if I wanted to go in his room to watch telly and so I said yeah.

I got up and followed behind him and sat on his bed wrapped up in his blanket. He kept his distance and was talking to me about what was on the tv. After some time, he asked me if I knew what sex was, to which I said no. He then went on to explain that it was something that people who loved each other did with each other, mainly boyfriends and girlfriends but other people could do it too. As I didn't know what it was, he was going to have to teach me and then instructed me in what I needed to do.

Just lay yourself down a bit more he said and now I'm going to take your knickers off, which he did. He laid on top of me and took his penis out and said it may hurt a little bit, but I promise to try and be careful. He asked if I was okay at this point whilst I was unsure of what was happening, I thought I was as I wasn't hurt and although it was weird to my knowledge nothing bad was happening. Then he started to push little by little with each push his man-sized penis into my small 8-year-old vaginal hole and this was when it started to hurt and the more, he pushed the more it hurt. I squirmed and said ouch the more he pushed the more it hurt to the point of ouch actually coming out of my mouth. and he continued until I got too loud to which he then said does this hurt I said yes that must have been quite loud too because that was when he stopped and said that's what I had to look forward to when I was older, as that's what adults do when they get older and it's called sex and that's what sex is like, but it hurts you, so you won't be doing it, but it would probably be better then.. put your knickers back on and go to bed now. That's exactly what I did, and I laid quietly in the single bed opposite my little cousin's bed in pain not really having a clue what had gone on.

The next night when it was late and quite Tony came into the room again and started calling me, I didn't answer because there was no way I was going to watch tv with him again if that's what was going to happen. But he wasn't planning on giving up so easy because he ended up just coming into my cousins' room and kneeling by the side of the bed, I was sleeping in he tried shaking me to wake me and calling my name in my ear. Even at that point my not responding was not enough to stop him as he then put his hand under the covers and took my knickers and flung them across the room, I saw later they had landed next my cousins' potty. Suddenly there was the sound of a door and footsteps coming along the hallway. For some reason my aunt had got up. Tony flew up and went by the door and made it to the door just as my aunt arrived at it and asked him what he was doing. "Oh nothing, I thought I heard a noise, so I just thought I'd come and check on the kids make sure they were alright."

The next day a few of my aunts' friends came round Tony was feeling quite lively and had music playing and the back door open and trying to dance with all my aunts' friends who were finding it quite annoying as he was like being that in-your-face kind of guy. I went home that evening and don't even remember going back to stay there again and actually now as I sit writing this, I actually have no idea why that was.

Summer holidays came round, and it has been organised for me to fly to Grenada with Isiah and my step aunty, even though I had travelled before this is my first memory of being on a plane. I was so excited to be able to go on a plane again, especially after all that time watching them from the airport restaurants on my many trips with Patrick and Sylvia. I enjoyed watching the clouds and going through them as the plane went up in the sky and telling my step aunty how the people look like ants. With the flight being so long food was available, wasn't the best meal I'd ever had in my life, I still enjoyed the experience though as I've always been a foodie. Less enjoyable though when connected with things that aren't nice like when you're given a sweet and then your ears start popping.

When we landed, we were picked up from the airport by Mr. Man. It was like a whole new world out there, people driving around the rocky, uneven roads, some of which had edges next to long drops in their pick-up trucks with others running behind them and hanging off the back and then jumping off when they got near where they wanted to be. Our rocky road journey took us to a pink house with a veranda and rocking chairs outside. This is where Mr. Man lived with his wife who we called Aunty Man. I don't remember any full stories about our time there, but I caught a glimpse of a carnival parade and there was a lady that they called Nurse who lived diagonal across the road in a house that was painted green and had a cocoa tree in her garden and we often used to pass by. One day I ventured down a little further to see what else I could see and got scared. There was a lovely house with black iron gates curiosity was leading the way until two angry Dobermans came flying round a corner barking their heads off with drool flying everyway. Lucky for me they couldn't get out. But after that I knew when I had gone too far when I was playing the stick and wheel game. Not sure exactly what it was called but you just needed a stick and a tyre, and you rolled the tyre and kept control of it with a stick. When I got too close the dogs would start barking before I could even get to see the gate again. I guess it was almost therapeutic, the game that is. Not being barked at by the angry dogs that was scary. My favorite treat was a snow cone. I thought it was weird at first eating something from a plastic bag. But then there became something about biting the corner of the creamy ice filled flavoured bag and taking time to get through the contents.

We visited the beach on a few occasions one of which I was told the Bounty ad was filmed but upon some small online research this seems too not be true. Although this doesn't take away the fact that the beach was so beautiful. the things I found beautiful were the fireflies congregating randomly in a space for no reason lighting up the darkness of the night.

Late one evening whilst sitting outside of a bar with my step aunty whilst her dad, Isiah sat inside talking to someone, we were sat talking on the steps and having a giggle drinking when something giant thing flew passed our head and still till this day, I swear blind it was a spider.

My step aunty had family in St. Vincent, so we took a small flight on a small plane and there for a week, I don't remember much about my time here on this visit.

I enjoyed my time there, enjoyed meeting people and loved the weather, I was also intrigued by the people including children were walking around with no shoes on. I tried but it was very hot and uncomfortable. We took a trip to the beach and was told it was the beach where the Bounty advert was made and that made me love it even more. We also took trips to go down deep in the land, one morning after getting ready to go I put my foot into my wellington boot and got a bit of a shock as there was an insect in there that pinched my toe and boy did it bloody hurt. After getting over the shock and pain of it we took a nice long walk deep down into the land can't remember why we went but there was a massive downpour of rain which felt good as the rain was warm.

Night life was great, but I got freaked out on an early evening when Isiah took me and my step aunty to a restaurant bar. We sat outside whilst Isiah was inside talking. All was well until a big, massive insect came flying past my head, I froze and screamed when I wanted to run and scream. Never found out what it was but I'm fairly sure it was a flying spider. Isiah thought we were messing about though and shouted out "allyuh stop that noise".

Sitting on the veranda was a kind of peace listening to the crickets chirping like they were singing a song together with the fireflies acting like glowsticks, I hated the cock roaches though. Even more so when me and my step aunty went to visit her family in St. Vincent for a week. We took a flight on a little Fiat plane from Grenada, it was only an hour away. I was having a shower minding my own business and flung back the curtain to get to see a carpet of cockroaches' covering the Lino on the bathroom floor. Boy did I scream. My step aunty's cousin came flying in with the cockroach spray and then we waited patiently until they had dispersed enough for me to have a safe enough path to come out of the bathroom.

When we arrived back in England, life seemed quite with lots of hush hush conversations and although they were probably not connected as it was something that happened anyway, it later transpired that they were. Lots of trips to the sweet shop to get quarter bags of sweets were happening too, Midget Gems, Pear Drops and Rhubarb and Custard were top of the list. I also remember eating a hot banana crunch dessert too. I often wish for them to bring it back, but it probably won't taste as good as I remember it as with most food s these days.

Haven't got a clue what the time frame was, but I was asked the question about how I felt about going to live in Grenada, I now know that this what the conversations were about. Initially I wanted to go because it was hot, and I liked that, but I was also put off by off by the pinched toe incident and the flying spider. The next conversation was about who I wanted to live with if I had to stay in England. My first choice was with my aunt as I was closer to her then than I was my mum and staying with my step aunty and two uncles wasn't an option. Staying with my aunt was ruled out straight away which I had mixed feelings about as I hadn't seen Tony around so didn't feel my being with her was any cause for concern. There was talk about going to live with my dad, but my nan wasn't having it she said he did too many drugs, even though he did less drugs than my aunt because he only smoked weed. Then I was asked what about my mum and how I felt about staying there. I also had mixed feelings about this as even though she was my mum I didn't really know her. Being sent to visit my mum

became a regular thing I would walk there by myself, and it was fun at first but then things started to happen like her arguing with her boyfriend and his girlfriend's daughters coming to the flat to argue which led to my mum spraying hair spray in her face through the letter box. And getting beat seemed to be a thing too and at those times there I couldn't even tell you why that was happening. The fact that I'd only ever been beat once with a belt once before was definitely a big shock to the system.

The worst that had happened during growing up with my nan and her husband was when he asked, "do you like apples, do you like Pears and do you like falling down the stairs?" I answered yes to the first two and no to the third but got pushed anyway. And another time Isiah left me money from the tooth fairy underneath the Vaseline pot on the dressing table because he couldn't get to the pillow as I always slept by the wall and my step aunty by the edge. Id' been on my own all day and when my nan got home, I was all excited and showed her the money. When she asked where I got it from, I said the tooth fairy, but she didn't believe me and went mad and started calling me a liar.

I don't know how the decision was made or what was agreed, I vaguely overheard something being said about my mum not wanting to have me unless she got some money. But I still ended up being there, to be fair I think the money in question was my child benefit, which she would have been entitled to but who knows.

She lived on the opposite side of the school nearer the entrance my brother left from, in a block of flats. It was a nice community area; I knew that from when I used to visit. The flats were set out in a square shape with a concrete area in the middle and an old people' s home on the other side. To the right of that was a two-plank fence which you could climb through if you walked up the slope walkway by the pub as short cut to get to the flats and at the bottom. All the children who lived in the blocks got along so it was great fun with our favourite game being forty, forty save all. Behind the flats on the left was a fire station so we often saw the trucks when they left the depot.

The flat was a two bedroom my mum had the biggest room with brown wooden mirrored wardrobes and her bed with her favourite spread, the

Pierrot, and her wicker chair in the corner. My brother and sister shared a room not only with each other but also with Paw - Paw. He was always a source of topic at some point. Luckily for them they didn't have to share a bunk bed with him as he was only a giant dog teddy with dungarees. The kitchen was small with a view of the field in the distance and the petrol station across the road. Spacious enough to get the job of cooking and washing done but not really spacious enough to have more than two or three people in there. The bathroom was like a box with pink and white shell wallpaper. The living room was a nice size, very cosy and perfect for entertaining I don't remember much about the furniture, but I do recall a black shelving unit that had a few collections of books on. One set was called how my body works, which we collected each week with a different body part to put a skeleton together and each book had detailed descriptions of internal body parts and picture of them. The other collection was a children's encyclopedia collection called Childcraft.

We didn't stay there long when after I moved in not even sure I know how long we were there for. My earliest memory of being there was getting beat with a leather belt, it was my first experience of getting beat by my mum and it burned after all the beating and screaming crying and shouting that went on soon stopped, I was in the bathroom putting chilly water on the wale marks that were left behind from the lashes of the belt.

We were soon in a three bedroomed house on a corner with a garden which we enjoyed having and the kitchen had a hatch where our mum often passed our dinner through when we were sat at the dining table which was at the back of the living room. We weren't here for too long, but it was good here other than having to count pennies and scramble change for me and my brother to be able to get the bus to school as we still went to the same one. At this time, I had started to spend more time with my biological dad who would come and get me on weekends which was always good unless he had angry outburst. One day we pulled up in his silvery blue Volvo, not quite outside of the house more at the back of the house he was in an argument with someone which I guess was some form of road rage thing. I sat in the car whilst he got out leaving his door open and walked round to his boot where he took out a baseball bat and began to fight. I have no recollection of how it all started or who stopped it. I did later learn that he was stressed and having a challenging time as had recently had a baby with his now long-term girlfriend, the baby was born with a cleft lip and pallet. I overheard him talking about it to my mum it was the first time I saw them in a room together let alone talking.

We then moved again to a place called Maidenhead, my mum had done an exchange. I shared again with my sister and my brother got to have his own room which he was incredibly pleased about. He had his room painted blue with blue curtains and myself and sister had a pink room with pink curtains, which were genuinely nice but I hated that they let the light in on summer nights and so you could see the shadows of the other children still playing outside whilst I was tucked away in the top bunk by 8pm. It fell through one night when I was making it up, not sure who put it together, but it had been the wrong way, luckily my sister jumped from her bed through the gap at the head end and made it out before I could land on her.

We had an end house on a Cul-de-Sac right next door to a massive field which was sometimes used to play football and a play park adjacent a basketball court. Young and old would either walk through there or play here. One route would take you to the library and town. Another route through there took to you towards a bus stop and school and a third route led you to another road with housing and towards a main road.

Summer times were best, we all gathered to play rounders or were allowed out late us young ones would sit and have a drink and those who smoked, smoked. Before we all got to doing those kinds of things, we kept ourselves to ourselves until we all got to know each other. Our first encounter of the area was my brother having his bike nicked, our mum sprang into action and sprinted so fast to catch up with the boy and get the bike back. The next whilst doing more unpacking I was stood in the garden having a break when I was approached by a girl who lived across the road. She asked if she could ask me a question to which I agreed. The question was "so you know like how you can get and salt and pepper. Are you salt or are you pepper?" I replied saying "that depends on what pepper you mean because there is white pepper and black pepper" I could feel myself smiling inside as I never even knew about white pepper until eating a meal with Patrick and Sylvia because Patrick used to have it on his Sunday roast. That deterred the conversation for a moment or two because she was unaware of white pepper. She then bought the conversation back to what she wanted to know asking if I was white pepper or black pepper. To which I replied black. She had seen black people before but hadn't spoken to them and said she had asked because she knew I was different to the people round the corner. The people around the corner were from Pakistan but when they were arguing with each other they would shout and swear and call each other 'black pakis' which I never understood but I never asked we all just used to leave it between them. Everyone in the Cul-de-sac who socialized got along so there was no cause for concern.

Before friendships grew, I went on a walk with my little sister and a girl from the estate who was kind enough to walk with us and show us the way. All was going well until on the way back she ran off with my sister and hid. It was dark and we were still quite new to the area, so I had no idea where to look and had no idea where they had gone. They went quite far and hid round a corner and kept quiet and still. The more I called and the more I looked the more panicked I became. I was filled with dread at the thought of not being able to find my sister and having to go home without her and say she is missing. My mum was big on us taking responsibility for things no matter how big or small, so I knew losing my sister would be big trouble. When they jumped out at me, I completely lost it had a go at the girl and then slapped her in the face, grabbed my sister by the arm and frog-marched home and told my mum what had happened. She just said my name in despair as she felt I had overreacted. Maybe I had but nothing would have made up for it if things had of gone the other way. Looking back, I guess by this point I was already suffering with anxiety. The girl was shocked and confused and really quite upset. As she didn't understand why I was so angry as her intentions were not to upset and scare me it was just a joke. Unfortunately, I didn't take it that way. Once she had a calmed down which took a few days I explained how I was feeling, and she understood and from there the friendship bloomed along with many others.

The house became a home and we started primary school. We went to a place called Larchfield, it was a little way but quite a nice little place with red and white uniform. After a few months here and a break for the summer holidays I was soon at a new school called Altwood secondary school in year 7 with our mint green and black uniform. My brother was still at Larchfield, and my sister started at St. Edmund Campion which was a catholic church school next door to the school I went to.

My mum was initially brought up as a Catholic, so this was quite fitting for her. Once my sister had settled in and had her holy communion things went well. Before this she had issues with falling asleep in class. As I did the school run the teachers would pass things on through me as my mum was at work. I always answered as best as I could and was sure to pass things on to my mum. The difficulty came when they discussed their concerns about my sister falling asleep in class. They wanted to know if she was well and how well things were at home as she seemed to be falling behind, because she kept falling asleep in class. The final issue raised was "well we also wondered if it is because of you know" she said with a nodding gesture I looked her with a frown and confused look. Again, she said, "you know because of." With me still not having a clue she went on to say because of how we are different and because of where we're from. At first, I was still a little baffled because we had come from a different town not a different country. Then thinking about the differences, it became obvious because the only difference other than the teacher obviously being older, I knew that wasn't it because that was to be expected so it had to be the skin colour. We clearly lived in a predominantly white area, it wasn't a thing for me but obviously it had been a thing at some point with the salt and pepper question I had been asked, me and my brother being the only black people in our Primary School and there only being three black people including me in the secondary school and my mum being the only black person at work. It was clearly a thing, a thing that I had noticed but not made a thing of and other than out of curiosity neither had anyone else up until this point. I assured the teacher, although it may have been quite abruptly that there was nothing wrong with my sister and that she had been able to read even before she started school and was more than capable of doing her work. I reported back to mum as soon as she got home, and she then took the situation in hand. It turned out that my sister had an iron deficiency.

CHAPTER 5

It was funny moving in with them as it felt like I had moved in with strangers, but I just had to take each day as it came. A few weeks after we had moved into a house in Maidenhead the back garden was more like a jungle than a garden made more real by the fact that there were often snakes in the grass. Moving day was rather eventful with my mum crashing the moving truck into the bridge with no serious outcome. Once it was all decorated and we sat down in the living room on the funky purple coloured patterned sofa, where our mum spoke a few, brief but important words to us. Those words were, if in anyone touches you anywhere in anyway then come and tell me no matter who it is. It seemed an odd thing to say but we didn't ask any questions we just agreed and got on with our day.

After some time, we started to get a visit from a family member. I had seen his face before, but I didn't really know who he was. My first recollection of him was when I lived with My nan and Isiah. I was on my own in the living room when he came in., he said hello and asked where everyone else was. I answered and then he looked away. Our living room was a funny shape, but this part of the living room had the sofa with stairs behind it but with a gap in between as a walkway. Opposite the front of the sofa was the tv on a ledge inside like a cubby. On the right side that stretch of wall there was a gap where he stood, and I rolled around on the floor. Other than looking at me to ask the question he asked he made a point of not looking at me. Just trying his best to keep his focused fixed on the other side of the living room. I was quite a chatty child at times so I rambled on and told him that I had been seeing how long I couldn't go to the toilet for and that I managed to go an entire day. He said, "oh that's not good I think it's probably better if you go." I think I was desperate at that point so decided to go. I know now why he was trying not to look at me and why my rolling around on the floor was making him feel so uncomfortable.

The funky purple sofa

The second time I saw him was at our house in Junction before we moved to Maidenhead. He was tall and big with a little head a bit like how you would imagine a monster to be even though he didn't look like a monster to me at the time. He had large features and was very loud with a stammer and when we moved to Maidenhead, he was always there buying things like chestnuts at Christmas and takeaways and turning up with like cakes and sweets. This time, he just stood in front of the fireplace a bit like he did before but differently as we weren't alone, my mum and siblings were there. Although, I do remember wearing a white dress with black spots that my mum had given me and him telling me that I shouldn't wear that, I should be wearing something more covered up. As far as dresses go it wasn't even bad, it was knee length and flowed out at the waist with the top of it being like a vest but with a higher front and thick straps. After that I remember always wearing it with a shell suit jacket zipped up over the top. Turns out he used to live in Maidenhead before we moved there.

Me in the dress and shell suit jacket aged 10

I never thought for one moment that my mum would be referring to him when she made the comment of not letting anyone touch us in any way whatsoever. In fact, I didn't have a clue about what she might have been referring to. After this conversation we started to see a lot more of him. It wasn't directly after so I guess I should be fair to myself that the connection would not have been obvious. Also being 11 years old that would not be where my mind would have wondered to. Especially as he would come round and crack jokes, take us places and come bearing gifts. He became a regular to our household with no problems, so it became the norm.

Time passed and my friendships grew, in the summer we played rounders together as we lived next door to a massive field and play park, sadly that got put a stop to one of my friends got hit in the face with a cricket ball that we were using to play rounders with as we were out of tennis balls. There was also a club in the town centre called Escapades that put nights on for the under 18s we all used to go together. My mum enjoyed making clothes in her spare time and she chose me and some of my friends to model them for her at a fashion night that was being held at the after dark club. My mum always had a flare for being different so rather than just have us walk on and off the stage, she choreographed a dance for us to do on the stage. To the song Back and Forth by a well, known and loved female American artist. It went down really well, and my step aunt and uncles and their friends

spread your wings, speak your truth, write it down & let it   44
go

modelled some clothes too.

Amongst these good times my mum's older brother who we will call Ashbert became more of regular and began appearing at the house when my mum wasn't in. Nothing happened at first and on this occasion, I have no idea where everybody was and I was alone a lot of the time anyway, but we were in the kitchen just me and Ashbert. He was asking questions like where my mum was and how long would she be, and did I know when she would be coming back. I didn't know the answer to any of these questions. He then asked me to come and sit on the stairs, I asked him why and he told me not to ask questions and to do as I was told. I didn't know if he would beat me or not and didn't to take the risk and so did as I was told. We got beat a lot and for what I see as little things as well. But I guess it didn't matter how big or small what you did was if it was seen as wrong you were punished. I have been beaten for eating Nesquik, using more bread than I should have, using too much sugar to the point where my mum would get sugar sachets and count out a certain amount for the tin. As we were only allowed two sugars in our tea she would know if we used more. And with the bread she started to count the slices and write the number of how many were there before she went to work. So, we would have to account for every slice we took. Me and my brother got beat so much that one time our little sister felt left out so she asked if she could come and join the line-up. That's the part where we would have to stand next to each other whilst being questioned about who had touched, said, or done something. That was after being sent to choose the belt that we were going to get beat with. There was no point choosing a little one as we would get beat for that too. At times my mum already knew who needed punishing, but she would still go through the line - up process. The windows would get closed and then the curtains to reduce to the chances of us being seen and heard. I don't think that the things we got beat for required the beatings that we got. Every time social services would turn up; they would listen to what my mum said and then leave and then we would get into trouble for calling them. My mum told us that's how she was brought up and so she was doing what she knew

For the reason of not wanting to be beat I did as I was told and went to the stairs where with no hesitation, he pulled down the bottom half of my clothes and put me on the stairs, I asked him what he was doing and told me not to worry about. He spread my legs open, and I told him that I didn't want him to do this to me and he told me it was tough he was going to do it anyway. And he did he forced himself on me and in me until he ejaculated. I attempted to get away, but he grabbed my hands and put them together wrist to wrist and gripped them together tightly in one hand whilst he forced his penis in and held me down with the other. Not only did I have to endure this oversized man inside me and on top of me I also had the stairs digging into my back. The front door was opposite the stairs, and I wished for my mum to just appear at any moment, she literally would have walked in on her brother raping her child. He went through the kitchen which was to the left if you were facing the stairs and went to the bathroom which was by the back door and got a flannel and wiped my now 11-year-old vagina. He told me to pull up my clothes and he fixed himself up. I told him I didn't like what he had done, I would have preferred to have been beat. He told me that he didn't care. I told him I would tell my mum and he told me I wouldn't because he knew I feared her and that she wouldn't believe me anyways and if I did, he would do worse to me than he already did. That was me silenced by the truth and threats. He left and I went to my room and stayed there 'til my mum got home. After this, I did whatever I could to avoid him whenever I could sadly this wasn't always possible, therefore he raped me whenever he could. Ashbert clearly liked what he was doing as he had arranged for me and my brother to go and stay with him and his daughter, our cousin. She lived in Reading and her and my mum were close and so we saw my cousin even on the days that her dad didn't have her, when he did, he brought her round. It was during a school holiday, so we were there for what seemed like more than a lifetime, but I think was only a week. He lived in a cottage up north we spent the daytimes alone making food and watching tv. But at night he would have us all in his bed. I would have to be on the edge so he could have easier access to touch me without the others knowing. I'm not sure if he ever tried it with his daughter but she was always loud and fidgety and was confident in making a scene. He would be in between me and his daughter and my brother lay by the wall. Even though he touched me inappropriately whilst we stayed with him, he never had the opportunity to rape me. His daughter made too much of a fuss and asked far too many questions for him to try and get away with anything one night she annoyed him so much that he got out of the bed and went to sleep in the other room.

My relationship with my mum was still not great as we still hadn't really bonded nevertheless, I still did a lot for her. I would cook for us all when we got in from school and on the weekends, I would also have to do the housework. I even pretended to not be my mum's daughter once when she started dating and she wanted to bring a guy to meet us, she wanted to me to say that I lived next door and was the babysitter. I agreed at the time partly because I felt as though I had no choice but also because I wanted us to get along because on the rare moments, we did it was good but overall, I never really knew how to take her. As a result of this I'm sure you can imagine confiding in her was not something I was able to do. I spoke when I was spoken to and only really asked for things if other people were there as I knew her attitude would be different. When others were around, she was seemed more lighthearted and friendly. This wasn't always the case though if she wasn't in the mood for something or was pissed off you certainly knew about it. On occasion some people did challenge her from time to time. One day I felt so humiliated by her, and friend asked her how she would feel if I got up and slapped her in the face. My face changed and spoke, and she took one look at me and told me to not even think about it. But I did and I did on many occasions but most of the time I was scared to even answer back let alone anything else. I had surprisingly plucked up the courage to call social services and Childline to no avail as it just led to us getting into even more trouble. Social services would come and confront my mum she would get angry tell them all about themselves and slam the door in their faces. They would leave and we would get cussed and even beat when she was sure they were gone.

My most violent rape was one of the ones that haunts me the most was during the Christmas holiday, 31st December 1992; we had had a nice Christmas and my mum was able to get me some nice things to wear and use rather than things I needed. I got a high neck jumper which had a black back and red and white diamond shapes on the front, I also got some beige jodhpurs and a pink curling tong. Family came to visit including Ashbert. I kept my distance and there was houseful so I felt like nothing could happen. This was going well until he concocted a story about his girlfriend. Apparently, she was meant to be coming to join us, but he couldn't get hold of her, and he said he was worried. He kept using the house phone to call her after several times he started saying how worried he was. He suggested he should go and see if he could find her. She worked in a nursing home in Surrey. He suggested taking someone with him and said he would be back with some food and in time for the new year countdown. Somehow it ended up being me and my brother going. I was told to sit in the front and my brother sat in the back. We got to the nursing home that he had the keys to. We went inside no one was at the reception desk and we walked down a blue carpeted corridor to some rooms, all the doors were orange. He opened the door to one room and told me to wait. He went off with my brother and put him in another room and came back. I told him he couldn't touch me because my brother would wonder where we were, but he told me he told him that we were helping a lady in with her shopping. He then said he had put the TV on for him so he would be fine. He told me to get undressed, but I refused so he did it for me I was doing my best to fight him off when he pushed me on the bed at this point, he was angry, so he was rougher than usual and dragged down my leggings and yanked up my bodysuit, so it popped open and pulled down my knickers and undid my bra. My vagina was already hurting from where he had been so rough but he didn't care was so busy being angry and keeping me in place by holding my wrists tightly above my head so he could do what he wanted. This time he forced more of himself in, this time it lasted longer, the pain was excruciating, and he was making sexual noises. At first my brain was moving from the pain in my wrists where they were tightly squeezed together by his one-man sized hand to the pain that he was inflicting on my vagina, the harder he pushed the further he went in causing me to cry out in pain. He looked at me and told me that I scream and cry all I wanted because no one there could hear me. Then he kissed me whilst rubbing my breasts. I felt so sick he didn't just a peck me here and there he actually full on kissed me on the lips and then started to put his tongue in my mouth and was just basically licking my mouth out. I started to feel suffocated on top of being in pain in my vagina and wrists and being crushed by his large body. At that point I just lay there not responding knowing that there was nothing I could do now and anything I had done to stop this hadn't made any difference other than making it worse. I believe that it was in this moment that disassociation became part of my life because I started to not feel any-thing and it was though I just wasn't there anymore. This time after he cleaned me up with a towel, he then cleaned himself up over the sink using water and the same towel. We went to get my brother and true to his word we stopped to get fish and chips on the way back and made it home in time for the New Year countdown whilst the song 'sweat' was playing on the radio. Now I was even more destroyed than I thought I could ever feel. It was from then onwards that the feeling of being dirty, that I had felt before from the inside out stuck with me.

He had been arrested and from what I have seen in my files from social services my family were hopeful that he would go down, as it turns out he is known for abusing others. My mum had requested a move and after the arrest had been made, she feared he would come to the house again. It was agreed that he had a threatening personality so for safety we went to stay in London with Levi and his wife and three children. I believe whilst we were there Ashbert called, or he called him it looked

spread your wings, speak your truth, write it down & let it   49
go

quite staged to me at the time. Regardless as to whether it was or not, he told him to stay away from us all. My dad was told and. As you'd expect he was very angry but was told by social services and the police to not get involved.

I had become so worn down, alone and gone into myself that I couldn't even see myself anymore, as it happens, I'm not even sure if I knew who I was to know what to see and everyday just became about going through the motions. If someone thought it was weird that I didn't go out I went out, if people commented on me not speaking, I would speak. and I started to do everything I could to avoid people I think subconsciously as well as consciously. Every time I was raped or touched this got worse. I filled a bath and filled with Dettol in the hope that it would make me feel clean, but it never did, this feeling stayed with me well into adulthood no matter what I did. In fact, it made the situation worse because then I got thrush which led to me being talked about at school because it was so bad other people could smell me. My periods got weird and started to become browner rather than red. Not sure if any of this was connected but it was what I was going through at the time. Then I started to worry about being pregnant and didn't know what to do or who to speak to. My friends had noticed how different I was and continually asked what was wrong I always said nothing, but there were never satisfied as I was now always acting out of character. Tears began to flow, and the confrontation had led to an argument which is when it all came out whilst waiting to go to class. They took me to a teacher and sat with me whilst they explained what happened and I just confirmed that what was said was true. The school wrote a letter to my mum asking her to come in. When I got home, I gave my mum the letter that school had written but instead of reading it she insisted on me telling her what it was about and why she had to go into the school. As you went into the house and stepped into the hallway immediately upon opening the front door, the stairs were in front of you and to the left was the kitchen and to the right was the living room. My mum was stood on the step of the fireplace in the living room, and I had my foot on the bottom step and was unable to speak. Then I was looking at the stairs and then looking at my mum. She was looking at the letter and then looking at me and getting impatient she went from willing me to speak to shouting at to me to speak and then I said it "Uncle Ashbert has been forcing me to have sex with him." I had no idea about the word rape at this time, so I used the word that defined the actions.

In that moment I saw my mum in completely different light. The colour drained from her face and it was like her soul left her body and a tear just streamed down her face on one side and she could not speak. Just one single tear just fell from the corner of her right eye and that very same tear took it's time and slowly rolled down her cheek. As soon as it had finished falling, she stepped into action. She left the house and was gone for a while I went to my room and sat in tears not knowing what to do. Her best friend at the time soon came and she comforted me and told me not to worry and that everything would be okay and that it wasn't my fault. Other family members that I was normally close to came over. There were lots of talks going on that I wasn't party to, my mum went to the school, but I wasn't part of that discussion either. But I do know that the school hadn't acted accordingly as they should have called social services and they didn't. social services themselves were not impressed with the school either and sent them a letter.

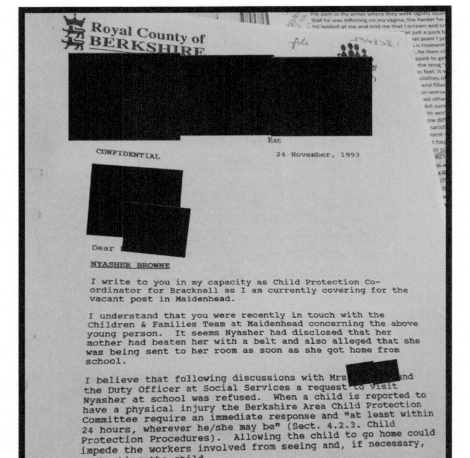

Royal County of BERKSHIRE

CONFIDENTIAL   24 November, 1993

Ext:

Dear

NYASHER BROWNE

I write to you in my capacity as Child Protection Co-ordinator for Bracknell as I am currently covering for the vacant post in Maidenhead.

I understand that you were recently in touch with the Children & Families Team at Maidenhead concerning the above young person. It seems Nyasher had disclosed that her mother had beaten her with a belt and also alleged that she was being sent to her room as soon as she got home from school.

I believe that following discussions with Mrs ███████ and the Duty Officer at Social Services a request to visit Nyasher at school was refused. When a child is reported to have a physical injury the Berkshire Area Child Protection Committee require an immediate response and "at least within 24 hours, wherever he/she may be" (Sect. 4.2.3. Child Protection Procedures). Allowing the child to go home could impede the workers involved from seeing and, if necessary, protecting the child.

I believe one of the issues involved concerned the matter of parental consent. I would in this instance refer to page 49 para. 3(b) of the Procedures which states that; interviews

spread your wings, speak your truth, write it down & let it go   52

- 2 -

24th November 1993

may take place in school in "certain circumstances (viz when a parent is the suspected abuser)." In the event Nyasher was not seen and returned home. When the worker called later in the evening she was not able to gain access. Had these injuries been serious or if the child was further abused as a result of an unsuccessful visit the consequences could have been serious.

I further understand that on a previous occasion a sexual abuse disclosure concerning Nyasher was not reported and handled by your staff, again contrary to the Procedures.

I am concerned that all agencies involved in Child Protection do work together to ensure that children are properly protected. Please be assured that any Social Services staff who undertakes an investigation has been trained and will handle the issue with extreme sensitivity. I do not believe this authority reacts to child protection in the manner that is sometimes reported in the media. I am sure you share my concern that such matters are properly handled and within the joint agency agreement through the Child Protection Procedures. In this connection I would be more than happy to visit you and your staff team to explore better channels of communication between the agencies to effect a united approach to Child Protection.

Yours sincerely

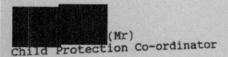

(Mr)
Child Protection Co-ordinator

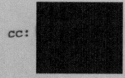

CC:

Care Manager/Supervisor, Maidenhead SSD
Senior Care Manager, Maidenhead SSD

AREAS OF CONCERN RELATING TO HOW SCHOOLS
HANDLE CHILD ABUSE REFERRALS

There seems to be no consistency, e.g.

1. When Nyasha complained at school that she had been sexually abused by her uncle, her tutor simply wrote to Miss Brown asking her to go into school to discuss something. Until Miss Brown spoke to Nyasha's teacher she had no idea what it was about.

2. The school made no contact either with the police or Social Services regarding the alleged sexual abuse. Miss Brown contacted the Police, who in turn approached Social Services when a joint investigation took place.

3. When Nyasha complained about punishment from her mother, her tutor at school contacted Social Services and then refused to allow Nyasha to be seen at school.

4. Nyasha told me that her tutor said, on the following day that she had not intended Social Services to be involved, but that she wanted to discuss the incident with Nyasha's mother.

It seems that there is some confusion at Altwood School about the procedures when dealing with child abuse/child protection issues.

████████ (Mrs)
Social Worker (Care Manager)
19.11.93.

People were round all the time for a few days after that, then it was quite my mum was off work and I didn't have to go to school. I was told about having to talk to the police about what happened and having to be examined. The police came and picked me up from school in an unmarked car and out of uniform and they took me to the police station. When I first went in, we went upstairs, I stood by the window looking out over the fleet of cars and asking about the bright orange spot-on top of the police car and finding out it was so the helicopters could spot them when they're working together. I was sat in a room and was told that the interview would be filmed rather than written. Then the video link would be used if it went to court and if it was still required for me to speak in court it would done by video link. I was given teddies to use to help with the description and show parts. The officer was impressed with how well I was able to articulate and the fact that I was able to use the correct terminology to describe the body parts. Then it was time for my examination I undressed my bottom half and laid on the bed which was surrounded by police doctors and my mum. They made notes during the examination and after they confirmed that my walls were extremely damaged, and she showed my mum exactly where on the diagram they had whilst I got dressed my mum and her sister went into the other room where they continued to talk. The damage was bad enough that it was clear it was not caused by tampons or any other instruments that people may insert inside themselves. and because of that the case was did not go to court and I was told that he was given a caution. Ashbert denied the charges and the CPS said there was not enough evidence for it to go to court, even though there had been proof of damage to my vaginal walls. This was checked and noted by the police doctor. They also asked for the clothes that I wore that night. I got them out the cupboard that I had shoved them in, but they were no good because they had been washed which hadn't helped. I remember not planning on washing on them and shoving them in the back of a cupboard in my room, so I didn't have to look at them. Then I was plagued with fear about getting into trouble for not washing them and I knew my mum would question me not wearing it again as it was one of my favourite outfits. That then meant having to say what had gone on which would then amount to Ashbert carrying out his threats of what he would do to us all if I spoke out. They got washed in the end, but I still shoved them in the back of the cupboard in my room as I heaved at the sight of them. Thinking back to it I don't think he specified exactly what he would do. It was just more like "don't test me coz you don't wanna see what I can do" and "trust me you don't wanna see how much more I'm capable of". What he was inflicting was pain enough in more ways than one, so I guess I didn't even need specifics. During this period, my mum was also being investigated at this time for her treatment of me and my brother which was now finally being taken seriously.

I also learnt that Ashbert had a law degree, so I guess that went in his favour with helping him to get out of the charges.

Things did slightly improve between me and my mum for a little while but at times during the process of all that was going on she would question me about what had happened. At first it seemed as though she was listening but then she would start going mad and screaming and shouting at me and saying that I couldn't be telling the truth, and, on some days, she even went so far to say that I was liar. That hurt it hurt a lot. It left a peculiar feeling as I didn't think I could feel anything anymore but it's almost like you have a piece of heart for various things and as each hurtful thing happens it blackens up and doesn't work anymore. It was like she hated me but looking back I think everything was all too much for her. She had given birth to a child at the age of 16 to a 21-year-old man who used to beat her after she was brought up in home where there was domestic violence. Then moved to another home where her and her sister were also raped and sexually abused by Ashbert. It transpires that he did this to lot of other people too and not just in the family and not just to girls. I also learned that one girl was able to get her case to court but they threw her case out because she used to masturbate with candles so therefore could have caused damage to herself. And him having a degree in law meant he knew how to play the system. It seems that no matter what he was always going to get away with it unless he was going to choose a girl who was in a close-knit family that would have gone and reported things straight away. But they never do.

It was arranged for me to have some counselling within a group of other girls who had been in similar situations. I don't remember much about it just that we folded an A3 piece of paper into 4 and was asked to draw something in each box that represent something about us. I drew a picture of a beach in one box to show Grenada. After all the sessions had finished, we were given a bag of sweets each from Mars as the lady's husband worked there. Apparently after this I became more open and talked more about my emotions. I don't remember this but this what the letters in my file say. More time was spent with my aunty who had now moved to Woodley, one of her main concerns was around me having sex as she didn't want me to be afraid not to have it because of what had happened. Because sex is a beautiful thing when it's done properly with the right people at the right time. No one ever taught me though when that was or when it would be or how I would know or the fact that it is also an emotional activity not just a physical one. I learnt that the hard way by just venturing out and having sex people in the hope that I would find what she was talking about. Time came and went an I did my best to try and be a so-called normal teenager and I got a job babysitting. At first, I used to go by myself, then my friends used to come with me as the lady was happy for me to do that and we all thought it was great as we had a free house. On a night I was staying over she said I could have a party, I always looked after the children well and put them to bed when they were supposed to go. This is where I had my first consensual sexual experience with two different boys. The children had been fed changed and put to bed and a lot of people had left. Then it was just me and two boys left. We had all had a drink and we were sat chatting when the conversation turned to sex and then who was going to go first. The person who went first went home and I spent the whole night with the other boy. Spending the time together was what I enjoyed the most as the sex part I wasn't really there for I just laid there whilst they got on with it the only good thing about it was it didn't hurt. Even though I didn't know what it was what I was doing I now know that I was disassociating. I had learned to give my body away and be in an uncomfortable situation without being present. The lady came home and had asked me if I had had sex that evening. I didn't know what to say to her and she saw the look of fear in my face and held me and reassured me that it was okay if I did. After that we talked about it, and she gave me a packet of pills and told me to start taking them and told me that she would provide me with more and that whatever I did I was not to put the empty packet in the bin at home. Then the party I had at the house where I babysat came out. Everyone was talking about it and so the adults started to hear and then they started to talk about it. My mum came in telling me that she heard I had got off with someone, I denied it at first and then said I had but that getting off only meant kissing. To us it did but to her it meant a lot more. She was right I had done more but I was scared because of how enraged she already was with what she had heard. She applied so much pressure that in the end I crumbled and told the truth about having sex. I was due to babysit again and hadn't gone because I wasn't allowed to, the lady came to my house looking for me and knocked the door to find out why hadn't turned up. My mum told the lady that I that I wasn't coming back and had a go at her because by this point my mum has concluded that the contraceptive pill packet, she had found in the bin was mine. I used protection with one but not with the other. My mum was so angry with it all she just lost it and started punching me. This finalized my decision to go with my dad this had become a discussion after the whole Ashbert situation, in the beginning I was in two minds as mine and my mum's relationship always seemed like it was gonna be okay then it would go bad again. A few days after this whilst I was washing up in the morning, I started being sick. My mum saw and said I wanna hope I'm not pregnant, she also been keeping track of my monthly's which I was unaware of until we went to the doctors after Ashbert raped me because I had been having my periods had become irregular. So now it was back to just chillin' in the park for the rest of the summer if I was ever allowed again.

CHAPTER 6

We never saw much of Tony for a while, until this same summer I found myself having to go there with my brother. I am not sure how I felt about this as I wasn't going alone, and we would be staying not just with him but also with his girlfriend and his two children, so surely things would be okay. And this was about 2 years after I had reported Ashbert. Even though there wasn't the right outcome anyone would think that he wouldn't want to go through the process, I guess he was thinking I wouldn't bother saying anything as Ashbert had still basically got away with it.

The layout at Tony's was quite odd, he had moved to Southampton now and had a girlfriend called Chloe and they had children. You opened the front door into a hallway and a few steps along was a flight of stairs. At the top of the stairs was another hallway that led to the children's room. Left of the top of the stairs the hallway led to the kitchen passing the living room on the right and their bedroom was through the kitchen. For some reason I have no recollection of the bathroom. My brother was put in the bedroom with the little ones, and I was put on the sofa. It was an okay time in general we went out I made friends with the children who lived next door and Tony's older daughter came to visit for a day. Just as I started to feel somewhat comfortable, which I don't think I ever fully felt as a child, or even as an adult. He came into the living room during the night and tried the same thing he tried when I was a child. As a teen but still a child but feeling even more of a child in this situation I tried to do now what I tried then, when he tried to approach me the night after he first raped me. I tried wrapping up in the blanket tightly, holding on to it and keeping my eyes shut tight. But this time he succeeded in getting into the covers and into to me. He fought harder to get the covers off and made a joke about me playing hard to get. This time there was no one to save me as no one was keeping an eye, like my cousin had done when we stayed at Ashbert's. The children's bedroom was at the far side of the flat and what could they even do anyways. I asked why he was doing this to me as Chloe was in the next room, he said that she was boring because she was sleeping. None of this made any sense I clearly wasn't comfortable, I was distressed, he kept saying that I was alright and that I just needed to relax, but he continued to carry out what he was doing until he ejaculated. He cleaned me up with a towel, whilst telling me that I was better this time than I was the last time, he had a fag and left to go back to bed. This continued until we left, we were there for two weeks.

Having to find a way to cope with men more than twice the size of you, related to you and keeping a hold of you by your wrists above your head and getting angry with you anytime you try to escape and then forcing their man sized penis inside of you and them enjoying it, whilst I lay there grimacing and suffering in pain and lacking in any sort of strength on a regular basis is inexplainable within itself and is no surprise that disassociation becomes a thing and a solid part of who you are. No one in the world is built for this much trauma and it doesn't even stop here.

On my return home the role of trying to be a teenager was slowly becoming a thing of the past. It was all just too much. He drove us back from Southampton with a black Hi-fi unit that had a Kiss 100 sticker on it. He carried it in and out it in my room. I didn't use it to begin with and then my mum questioned why I wasn't using it. I didn't know what to say and just said I didn't know. Then started to use it, I even played her records on it when she was at work. She caught me out one day when she had called form work. I told her I wasn't, but she knew I was and just laughed it off. And nothing more actually came of it.

The process of becoming quite and withdrawn began very soon after my return home. My friends started to notice again so this time I just opened up without the arguing. They took me to the school nurse who called social services who then called my mum to inform her of what she had been told by the school. The nurse had shared her concerns about me seeming isolated other than my friends at school. Who I am so thankful for and thanks to Facebook have been able to reconnect with and thank for helping me. My mum called my aunty and told her and then called my nan. She had called her when I spoke out about Ashbert but this time she came over. I think it was because this time no one believed but only because he wasn't known for it. He had been in prison once before but that was for burglary.

My nan came over to get to the root of what was going on and during her stay she decide she wasn't happy, not only with what had gone on but also by the way I was still being treated. I couldn't go anywhere for ages without anyone questioning me about what had happened and when and how. Then the words came "well why would he do that to you when his girlfriend was in the bed with him in the next room."

I had no idea how I was supposed to answer that I barely understood anything myself. His girlfriend was told, and she decided that she would have heard him get out of bed.

I spent a lot of time with my nan and plaited extensions in her hair for her whilst we also talked about what had happened. I then later overheard my nan on the phone saying that she believes me.

My nan spotted the distance in between me and my mum and wasn't happy with the differences between me and my sister in the way we were being looked after. My nan started meeting up with my dad. He knew what had happened with the rape sand was angry and disgusted at what had happened. When he and my nan met up, they talked about how things were for me in the house and together they decided that my dad should take custody of me. This so that I would be kept safe so nothing bad could happen again. More talks were had, and I even had one with my mum where she told me that my dad was no good. I didn't know how to take what she was saying. She explained a little about how he had mistreated her and how when I was born, he wasn't really interested in me and almost got her thrown out of her bedsit by kicking off at a party and threatening someone with a knife. She went to say how he always gave my older sister better things than he gave me. She gave an example of when I needed a coat it was only £3.00 but he told her he didn't have any money for it. That same week she saw my sister in town wearing a new coat which he had paid for that had cost £7.00. I didn't like the sound of this but and so part of me thought she was just saying things to stop me going. Then I thought well at least maybe she does want me.

From my files it showed my dad had tried to get custody of me many times. At one point he even went as far as turning up at my school and trying to take me form there, but the school didn't let him. I didn't see it happen, but I heard about it, and it has also been noted in my file. He was never successful in his endeavor because I never wanted to go. He believed it was because my mum was pressuring me to say no but the truth is whilst she did have her say I was always naturally feeling stuck and confused. This time he had my nan on his side, she had called my mum out on a lot of the things she had seen, and my mum had her answers. Initially my nan had come to stay with us from September to October but after having enough of my mum she went to stay with my step aunty in Reading but visited us every day. My nan used what she had seen to help my dad those things were,

The house was very cold

None of my friends were allowed round (my mum had said they were a bad influence)

I wasn't allowed out

I wasn't given any money to go to school with, but my sister was, (my brother was in care at this time).

My sister had a duvet and many blankets, but I just had a thin blanket

My mum was cutting my hair short like a boy even though I wanted long hair

There was little food in the house and generally the only meal we had was school dinners

My mum had a 2-hour cleaning job that she would send me to do

My nan had also left money with my mum for to go to Grenada, but my mum had spent it and made my dad pay.

After this my mum was seen by social services as evasive and erratic due to how she handled them and based on how she handled them before. My dad won the custody case and soon after that I moved. I felt bad for my sister, but I knew she would be okay as she always was. I feel like my mum protected her the most she was very funny about who was around my sister and who she let her be with. When lived together my mum said it was because we got to see our dads and my sister didn't really get to see hers. I just accepted that but there were some days when I just felt as though she was the favourite and most loved. By this point my brother was hardly at home he was in and out foster care and between our mum and his dad. Before all of that the last proper time we had together was when we went to Grenada with our step aunty, who I highly valued she was more than just an aunt to me I grew up with her until I was 10 and no matter where I was after that and what was going on she was always there. This time my nan and Isiah's house was built so we went to stay there this time. We went to beach where my brother was worried about sharks being the water. We enjoyed the sweet taste of snow cones, visited friends and family. Some of the days were spent with me and my brother taking the mace off of the nutmeg and leaving it on trays to dry ready to be taken to nutmeg plant ready for whatever they needed it for. We also made jokes amongst ourselves until one day my brother fully committed to some live entertains by tripping out of his flip flops. They were blue and yellow instead going between your toes they velcroid over the top. This day they didn't hold, and he went flying we laughed about it for days and still do now. Other days we would go in the land but not too far in. One day I attempted to brave it and go a bit further but me and my aunt came to a pit that a load of Congaree crawling around in it. We turned back and went home. Me and my step aunty went to visit her family in St. Vincent again for a week we went for a night out whilst she was there with her cousins. I began having abdominal pain whilst we were out, so we left the club and went to sit in the van until the driver took us home. Whilst we were waiting My step aunty's cousin went to KFC to get us some chicken. Those of us who were sat in the van waiting heard a motor bike come scrambling up the road and then a scream. My step aunty's cousin came flying back to the van in shock as it was here who had screamed as whoever was on the motorbike grabbed the bag of chicken out of her hand as they rode past. This was also the first time I had goats' milk which I have not liked ever since probably because it came straight from the goat into my bowl of cornflakes. Luckily for me we were running late for church that morning, so it was either eat it of go without. I went without.

Me at 14

Going to my dad's was weird and opened a whole new load of events. He was still with the same woman, who he had got with after being with my older sister's mum and he had three kids with her now, so they had moved from the flat to a house. So that's where we stayed. But then we had a chat and he explained that he wasn't supposed to stay there and that he had a room in a house that he was supposed to be living in. He paid whoever stayed in the room to go out so we could be in it when we had our visit from social services. I took a few of my things to put in the room to make it look more real that we were staying there. He told me what I had to say regarding the room and where we slept but left it up to me to answer the rest of the questions freely as he didn't know what else they may ask. I wasn't fully prepared for where we were going though, I don't think anything could have prepared me for it either. The room that he was meant to be staying in was in the same house that my aunt had lived in when I was 8. So now I was faced with having to deal with old emotions as well as having to remember to tell the lie correctly.

They came out and I followed the instructions I were given to me by my dad and there was a little confrontational moment as I had said to social services before about my mum shaving my head with the clippers. I don't think she did it to be spiteful but that wasn't how it felt at the time, and I hated it. She combed my hair up into an afro and ran the clippers over the top as a quick way to trim the ends. My hair was never the same after that. So, the social worker made a point of bringing this up as I had short hair at this time and when she first met me it was long. But that was because I had hair extensions then and now, I had taken them out ready to be done again, which I was able to do myself. In that moment though through my anxious state I was unable to articulate that and said it was just because I wanted it short now. I told my dad after the mistake I felt I had made, and he reassured me and told not to worry about it and then I started to feel okay. He was good at doing this and making me laugh. He felt I laughed a lot more than I needed to and asked if that was because I never really got to laugh at home with my mum. I didn't really have an answer, but it made me stop and think, then he was sorry for stopping my over laughter as it had changed how I was in that moment. I was starting to enjoy my time here as it seemed like a true family household.

We never stayed in the room we slept at his girlfriend's house, she was very accommodating, and I shared a room with my little sisters with two single beds pushed together. A few nights in I felt this excruciating pain it was a pain I had never felt before in my life in the end I was crying and crying. My dad and his girlfriend heard me and came to see what was up. I explained I didn't know and that I just had stomach pains that I had never had before. His girlfriend gave me something for the pain and some water to take it with and settled me back to sleep. I slept well into the next day waking to go to the toilet and most definitely was not expecting the shock I was given when I got there. There was something I had never seen before just lying there in the seat of knickers. I called for my dad's girlfriend, but she didn't hear me feeling cautious of the door being open and the fact I was sat on the toilet with me knickers down and my other brother and sisters being around I decided to shut the door before I got into trouble. Still in shock and unsure of what to do and not knowing what it was I scooped it out with tissue and flushed it down the toilet. This was never talked about, and it certainly never made sense to me. I had been sick since that morning at my mums I packed and moved my stuff okay and was able to keep up in PE with step aerobics and in the gym with all the equipment, so I wasn't ill. So just got back on with things.

We soon had news of my dad getting temporary accommodation for us to live in until we were rehoused. The area was quiet, and the road was full us houses and one mobile home which we were given at the end opposite a park. At the back was some jungle looking mass, that was the garden, inside was so cold, so we were always walking around doubled layered and wrapped in blankets. At night we would put the electric heaters on, and we had two armchairs next to each other and would have hot chocolate in the evening whilst watching a movie or something on tv. When it was really freezing my dad would put the chairs together so we could cuddle up and keep warm. That was until he whacked his penis up against me and pulled down my knickers to ensure I could feel it. I froze so quickly and had no room to move. But felt the change and asked if he should put it away. I said yes and he said OKAY sorry I thought that was what you wanted. Even to this day I don't know why he would think that or why he would even do it not only just because he was my dad but also because that was part of the reason he took me from my mum, so I would not have to keep being sexually abused and raped. But now it just looks he wanted me so he could do the same. It doesn't make sense that he would try so hard for so long to take me from my mum and even go to the extent of turning up at my school in Maidenhead and try to take me from there without my mum's permission. Even though I knew he mistreated my mum his prior actions around me looked like he was a safe option. But instead, I trusted another who I should have naturally been able to trust but instead took steps to break that down. With that he let me go to bed. In the morning I was getting ready for school and had my music playing and LL cool J track came on Called 'Doin it'. A part of it says 'doing it, doing it and doing it well' my dad came in and told me that's what he wanted to do to me. I just didn't speak. Another song ruined that I could never listen to again but had to put up with it when other people played it because how do you tell your peers to turn it off because it reminds you of your dad telling you he wants you like that. When we stayed at his girlfriend's, I didn't have to worry about avoiding him as such as I just chilled with my siblings. When I made friends, I would go out whenever I could. It was surprising I was able to make any friends as my cousin had taken intense pleasure in telling everyone she knew in the school that I lied about her dad raping me. I gave my side to anyone who asked but I don't think I was ever looked at the same after that.

The nights we stayed in the mobile hut I did my best to seclude myself, so my dad didn't come near me and cuddles from my dad had become a thing of the past as he took that away by making them into something else.

We were soon given a two bedroomed flat in Southcote it was a much better place and people would come to visit us here. Sometimes I would go straight here from school and other days I would go straight to his girlfriend's house. Nights in the flat were different to when we lived in the mobile home for some reason when we were here, he tried even harder to abuse me. He would come in my room or call me in his and throw me on the bed and we would spend what seemed like a lifetime every time fighting each other he was fighting to get in me, and I was fighting to get him off and keep him out of me. Some nights I would succeed and some nights he would. That distance from inside me that I knew oh so well returned and the sick thing is he noticed it, discussed it, and talked about it with his girlfriend, and they decided to take me to have some counselling. I couldn't see how it was gonna help. I didn't feel like the first lot of counselling helped me but maybe because something happened again after it undid all the work that had been done. Not understanding that at the time I didn't see the point I going, not only that just to add insult to injury who goes to counselling for being raped and sexually abused whilst still being sexually abused?

This counselling session was vastly different, just me and one lady in a room talking about random things. I had no idea what I was supposed to say and the fact that my dad was still abusing at the time didn't help. I didn't have many sessions and don't even know how or why it ended.

Connecting with other members of my dad's family was a great distraction especially as it meant I got to stay in their places which gave me a break. Accept from when we went to our grans, we were always sent up to see our disabled uncle and he would always try to touch us inappropriately. We soon learned we could stay away from as he couldn't walk, so we were able to do as we were told by going to see him and keep ourselves safe by standing in the doorway. On days he was feeling strong or maybe determined is a better word he would shift along his bed and grab his aids to help him try and get closer to us but then we would just run.

I was also able to reconnect with my older sister, we would often go to town together and I got to know her friends as well as making more of my own. Although one of my friends didn't like my sister as they liked the same guy, I did my best to avoid their situation but was often

spread your wings, speak your truth, write it down & let it   69
go

dragged in on the odd occasion. One time the girl who was supposed to be my friend punched me in the face over it. the girl was little but loud and got away with bullying anyone in her path, even some teachers. We were walking home from school, and we stopped by the shops where she gripped me up and said she had heard I had been talking about her. This wasn't true, I had noticed she had swapped her ring the hand she usually wore it on and had put it on the hand that she wanted to use to punch me in my face. That was exactly what she did right in my left eye. As soon as I could I got away I did whilst other people who had seen told her she was out of order. I passed a house on the way and some people stopped me to see if I was okay but when I looked behind me her brother was there, so I said I was fine and kept on going. Her brother shouted to me if I said anything I would feel his fist too. So, I kept going I couldn't even see properly but soon made it home. After this I started going to school alone, until I started to meet up with my other friend Marissa. Marissa was a beautiful looking girl of dual heritage and wore hair in curly extension braids, she didn't like to talk about many things, but we were still able to build a friendship. I never saw her with anyone else other than her boyfriend or occasionally her mum and her sister. She never went anywhere without doing her eye make-up which was always really well done. she had a well-defined athletic build and a sharp jaw line and loved to wear wrap around skirts I didn't say what had happened when I got in and tried to stay out of my dad and his girlfriend's way so they couldn't see my face but my black eye was so big, and my face so swollen this was no longer possible and I ended up being forced by my dad to tell to tell him, he wasn't happy. He got ready and took me up to the girl's house who done it as she only lived up the road. The mum asked why I didn't tell, and I didn't have an answer and then the mum asked if I was scared or her daughter to which I answered yes. She was a known bully and even her friends feared her. My dad went mad and started saying to me what was wrong with me. I don't know what he expected. I had been bullied left right and centre pretty much my whole life at this point and any situation prior to this where I had attempted to stick for myself had failed, as

spread your wings, speak your truth, write it down & let it   70
go

people still did what they wanted to me anyway and no one had received any consequences for what they had done to me. Even when people started to believe me about Tony in Southampton, they couldn't even bring themselves to say anything at all, not even sorry. Even then they only started to change their mindset because another girl had spoken out about being raped by him which led him to do a disappearing act, once he heard the police were coming for him. He has been in hiding up until a few years ago when he appeared on my aunts Facebook with his info stating that he was in Devon. I soon blocked both him and my aunt.

Going back to the flat with Marissa became a regular thing as this helped to avoid seeing people, I didn't want to see on the way home.

My dad was beginning to get uncomfortable with his girlfriend spending more time alone, so we stopped spending less time at the flat which meant I was a bit freer from him. That was until his girlfriend went on holiday to St. Vincent well at least that's where I think she went as that's where she was from. Then it was just me and him and my siblings as always things were going well to start with. Then on a Saturday morning I was getting ready to do a strip wash. This was a regular thing where we would fill a bowl with water and a splash of Dettol and take it to our room with soap and a flannel to wipe our bodies over with. I had taken off my underwear but still had my nightie on when I heard him, my dad coming up the stairs. I moved the bowl and got back into bed to give myself some extra cover although at this point it didn't matter what I did or didn't do he was going to do what I wanted any way. He climbed over the foot of the bed and lay next me. He started to speak, and I thought this was going to be the end of all things as he started by saying sorry and then well the end was just heart crushing and that has been just as traumatising as what he was doing. His words were "I'm so sorry I've been doing this to you Ny, but I don't know what's wrong with me coz I know it's wrong, but I just want to know what you feel like inside" and as he said those last words, he swiped his hand over my knicker less vagina. Then he left the room. I didn't bother to get a wash after that and just got dressed. That dirty felling that I had felt all of them years ago had never gone away and clearly no matter what I did nothing was going to change and if at any time that dirty feeling was ever going to have gone away it would have been brought back. Now he had done something to me in every single place we stayed so now nowhere was safe.

His girlfriend got back from holiday and could see things weren't right and she started asking questions and this clearly annoyed him but when she could see his annoyance she stopped asking. I think all this time she was getting to herself was changing her and he didn't like it. He looked like he was keeping control of himself and then a few days later he just lost it and just went for her and completely battered her in the living room we left the room and ran upstairs, and all sat together. When he had finished beating her, he went out, she took that chance to grab together what she could of hers and the kids and left. I knew she had called her sister and was going to go there but she didn't say where she was going, and I knew she couldn't. We had really built a bond and I so desperately wanted her to take me with her, but I knew she couldn't and before she went, she did apologise for this and said she would take me if she could but because I am not hers, she couldn't and taking me would make him come after her more. I understood and watched her go and sat quietly in the chair until he came back. He came through the door and got angry again when he could see she had gone he got his phone and started making calls to find out where she was. We drove around Reading looking for her until we got to her sisters, her sister did her best to defend her, but I think my dad hit her too as he barged his way in. That night still ended up just being me and him and, in the end, I think she was left with no other choice but to just come back home. Everything was quiet and strange for a while and my dad was being hands on helping out and stuff, but we never went back to the flat for a while.

Stupidly I started to get to some sort of comfortable again and for a brief period of time I was just being a teenager, hanging with friends, going out, going to school, and talking to boys. After one school day me and friend Marissa went back to flat with some boys that we were friends with. I ended up having sex and me and the boy fell asleep and didn't wake up until gone 4pm. This meant I was late home, we got dressed and he waited for me so he could walk me some of the way. But our fate had been selected and we heard keys in the door. I told the boy to hide on the back balcony and ran back into my room. It seems as though my dad was one step ahead of the game and came in looking for a boy. I obviously denied that there was one there and after looking in my room he went to the back balcony and gripped up the boy and dragged him in and started pushing him, the boy managed to get away. Without a second though my dad took down the net wire and started to beat me with it and called me a dirty bitch and asked me what I thought I was doing sleeping with boys. When he had finished, he made me give him my key and dragged me out of the house as we got out, he gripped me up by clothes and leant me over the balcony and threatened to throw me over, we lived on the fifth floor. I don't even know what I said or if I even said anything or screamed or spoke or cried, I just know I feared for my life. He put me back down to my feet and turned round to lock the front door. We went to the lift and went down to get in the car he drove angrily back to his girlfriend's house and told her he had caught me with the boy and that he had hit me. I went to the room I shared with my sisters and sat there. I could hear I was being called and reluctantly went downstairs and was asked if I wanted an ice cream. I must have had a confused look on my face, and he said" it's okay it's done now, and you have been punished so if you want an ice cream you can have one" so I said yes please. I went back upstairs until it came and then when they came back from the ice cream van with it, I came and got it and went to go back upstairs when I was told I didn't have to. It's just what I was used to from when I was with my mum. We would get shouted at beat and shouted at whilst getting beat and then sent to our room.

When I got to school the next day, the boy was looking out for me and asked me if I was okay and gave me a hug. I told him what happened when he left and that was the end of that, but we still spoke.

It wasn't over though, me being punished because when we went to the flat again, he started to try and abuse me again. This time he was more determined and was angrier with it and saying "oh say so you can give it away to little boys but not to me yeah" all whilst trying to get my clothes off and get my legs open so he could penetrate me.

CHAPTER 7

In the morning I took myself to school as normal and that day I never went back. People could see there was something really wrong I confided in my friend Tessa who I chilled with out of school. Tessa was of dual heritage with a brown tone and had a little round face with a prominent nose. She had long black hair that she always wore her hair in a bun finished off with a scrunchie. She had a lot of friends and was easy to talk to, we were always able to have a laugh and a joke, alongside deeper conversations that would stay in your mind long after the conversation was over, and we shared artistic skills. Even my bully friend wanted to know what was wrong she couldn't get anything out of me but I gave Tessa the permission to tell her so she could get the girl off her back. When Tessa told her, that was it my bully friend grabbed me by the arm and dragged me to the head of year and said what had happened to me. After sitting and talking through it with the teachers they called in the police and social services. Non uniform officers came into the school and took statements and made it clear that I could not return which I never really wanted to do anyway. They struggled to find a placement for me and asked friends if I could stay with them. Tessa's mum wasn't okay with it because she didn't have enough room. Marissa's mum agreed although it was reluctantly and I'm sure she soon came to regret it when she got a knock on the door in the middle of the night. It was my dad's girlfriend and his sister and asking what was wrong with me and asking how could do I this and why would I say these lies. To this day I do not know how they found out where I was and how they found out where Marissa lived to be able to knock her door in the first place. Social services were informed, and it was made clear that I couldn't stay there again. That night I cried myself to sleep and went to school the next day in the same clothes.

I had to go to the police station to make a formal statement and my head of year took me as my supervised adult. The woman that we had all feared so much and hated getting at shouted at by had become this down to earth supportive woman. It was so weird but funny weird we would have chats in her office but when the time was required, she would slip out of her office and become the shouty woman who was always telling people to tuck their shirts in and to walk in the corridor. She also sat with me in the social services office whilst they did what they could to find me a place. They contacted one of my step uncles neither of them had ever touched me or mistreated me in any way whatso ever. But I was told that he had said he was scared to take me in incase I accused him of doing the same thing. Which didn't make sense to me because unless he was gonna do that then why would I say that. Since reading my notes I have come to find that my mum didn't believe me either. She says she thinks I just said it to get out of there because I saw that he was stricter than I thought. There's a major difference between being strict and being abusive. No one seemed to have a logical explanation as to why I would be lying. I certainly wouldn't have been benefitting from it because the more I spoke out the more people I lost and the more alone I became. My aunt didn't want to take me in either because she was about to get married and didn't want me to say that about her future husband either. From where I'm standing that would mean to me that the man you were about to marry wasn't a good option because of what he was capable of. The most baffling thing of all is that my mum and aunt wondered why I left it so long to "blow the whistle" it says yet they have never blown the whistle on their own experiences. And to add to that when I saw one of my dad's friends who used to own a record shop on Oxford Road he told me that my dad told him I wasn't living with him because I thought I was too much of a woman to live with him my mum was annoyed that I didn't tell him what had really happened and that was after her telling me not to tell anyone what happened to me because other people use it against you or think they can do it to you too. The notes also go on to say

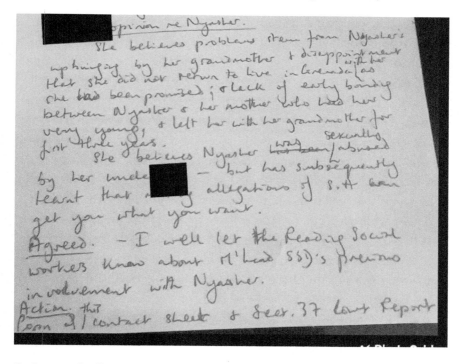

So just to clarify I was never promised to be able to go to Grenada. I was told that if I decided to stay in England then I would have to stay here but I would be allowed to visit. Making allegations never got me what I wanted because I sure as hell didn't want any of this. All I wanted was to be loved and treated well which I believe shouldn't have to be an ask as a child it should be given naturally. When it isn't it impacts all parts of life and filters down through generations until someone is able to break the chain and fix it.

They called foster homes some people refused some people weren't home and so we had to wait for them to get back to us. Whilst we waited for people to return calls, I was placed in a care home as a temporary measure until a foster placement was found but one never was. Anyone who had a husband, or a son didn't want me in their home. At the time I was told by someone it was because of what I had been through, and the people were concerned because of the outcome of my cases. No one being sent to prison somehow meant that what I was saying couldn't be true. I have since learnt from my files that it was because of sexualised behaviour. Not that I had a clue what that even was back then. But what happened to children learning what they are shown. So far in my 16 years of life at that point I had been shown to eat, how to cook, how it was to not eat, to be alone, and no matter who someone is they will take what they want from you when they want it and no matter what you say you will be considered a liar. Surely the best thig they could have done for me is to get me some help to change the sexualised behaviour and then place me somewhere safe. Maybe that was or Gods or the Universes way of showing I was safer in the care home because whatever behaviour I had none of the men in there did anything to me or with me that they weren't supposed to. There was a slight ray of hope come through that would have been good for me, they had found a black woman in Hungerford, but they then came to find that she had a 21-year-old sone so I couldn't go there either. So, there I was stuck in a room in a house with adults and peers I didn't know, with nothing but the school uniform I had on my back. They were friendly, but I didn't really say much I didn't have much to say and didn't think I'd be there as long as I had ended up being. I still went to school most of the time and was taken in by a woman's only taxi service. My hair needed doing again as it was looking rather picky. I used some of the grant money I was given to get some new extension hair I so could redo it as did my hair myself so that saved money. I had finished it in time to go to school, so I didn't go in. The care home wasn't impressed and told the school exactly why I wasn't there. When I did go back to school my head of year discussed this with me and I explained it was because I didn't get it finished. She explained that whilst it looked nice my education was more important than my hair. But to me getting my hair done was more important as it was one less thing to bullied about. Not that anything stopped my bully friend and whilst I was grateful to her for getting me away from my dad, she then got me suspended from school by stealing cheques from the music department and ripping them up and putting them in my bag. I was called to the office and allowed for my bag to be checked and there they were, in my bag. I told her I didn't know they were in there as I didn't take them. But because that's where they found she said she had no choice but to expel me. Which makes no sense because who does something like that and then willing goes to allow their bag to be searched knowing that what's in question would be found. Another person in my life who had shown support but when it came down to it didn't believe when they should have. I was allowed into school for my exams and that was it. That seemed pointless though because sitting in a room full of silence made it harder for me to focus and anything that I was meant to have learnt had not gone into my head. They did also allow me to go on the Alton Towers trip before we left. I was glad when school had finished as I was the only person in the care home who went to school, this had been another reason the home pushed the social workers to find me a placement in a foster home, they were worried that the culture of the care home wouldn't be good for me and have an impact on me not finishing school. Leaving school gave me more time to spend with the others and get to know them more and the people who had left and rehoused in their own places as they used to come back and visit. Three days after being there a few girls lent me some clothes as I had nothing but my uniform, so I was grateful for that they never judged me or made feel unwelcomed.

The social services went to my dad's house to try and get my things, but he refused to let them have any of it. This was when I started to drink, I had drunk before as I was allowed alcohol at parties and special occasions when I lived with my nan and Isiah. But I had never drank like this before, but this was our trend whilst being in the home. Finding people to buy drink for us getting drunk playing loud music and inviting people in that we weren't supposed to. The first night we did that I slept with someone, and I hated it, I don't even know why I done it and to make matters worse I didn't even like him. He wanted it so I just gave it to him. I felt disgusting after I always did after sex even sometimes after with the person I was in a relationship with. At some point he assaulted me, my notes say he hit me in the back of my head. The police were called, I also managed to get a copy of police files and the write up of that is also in there.as I write this I am now thinking about all my other sexual experiences from this point onwards and it seems like the new pattern is being abused or disrespected in some after having it. So, one was satisfied by me given them sex or by taking it from me. I still had to be hurt in some way.

Later when we were all outside, I went to step out in front of a car I don't who it was, but someone stopped me and dragged me back on to the pavement. People kept an eye on me after that then we went inside.

CHAPTER 8

We would have to do our shopping with the allowance we were given, I had to budget that little more though because I wasn't allowed any extra allowance to get hair products which cost more than the products that other girls needed. I only needed an extra £7 as well I did my best to fight for this and had a lot of support from me key worker Andy as he hoped that I would be able to make a difference for all the black people in care so they too could get what they needed to take care of their skin and hair. Even now I think what a joke that a necessity had been considered a luxury. The keyworkers were never happy when I had used some of my food budget to my hair products, but I had no other choice. Once a month on a Thursday we would go out as a household to do an activity that we chose. We did things like going to cinema, going to the arcade or to the funfair. One trip to the funfair resulted in me being accosted by my older sister she approached saying she wants to have a word with me. She then asked why I said all those things about dad. I told her because they were true. She disagreed and so I questioned her and said okay then but why would I go through all that with mum to then go to my dad to then tell a lie about him and end up in a place with people I don't know. I don't remember how that conversation ended or who stepped in or if anyone even did step in, but I most definitely didn't enjoy my night at the fair.

I got close to the boy in the room next door to me, Drew and we would go out together to go shopping or to pop into town. He liked swimming but I couldn't and well still can't swim but I would still go with him and watch, and we would walk home together and then cook together and have our dinner together. Everyone thought we were cute. One evening whilst on our way back from swimming my dad was driving along the road behind us. Obviously, we didn't see him until he was next us and had wound down his window and started calling me. I said to Drew "oh my gosh that's my dad." Drew knew what had happened and he said to me it's okay just hold my hand and hold it tight and just keep walking and that's exactly what I did. My dad was holding up the traffic but didn't care cars started beeping at him and I was ignoring him in the end he got mad and sped off. As soon as we got back home Drew took me straight in to the office and explained what had happened to the member of staff on duty. They called the police, but they said they couldn't do anything because he hadn't physically done anything to me in that moment. This happened on a few occasions and me and Drew holding hands whilst we were out became a regular thing. We were close to a degree for most of my time there our relationship became a sexual one until one day he was crying about something I went to comfort him, but he wouldn't let me close and then later I saw him crying in someone else's arms. That hurt, later he explained it was because things with me were too real and he couldn't handle that. With the others they just pretend they care in the moment and then get on with their own lives as normal after. We carried on being friends but stopped sleeping together but started working together on a market stall for an adult friend he had. That lasted for a few months when Drew then said his friend had asked a favour and wanted me to give him a blow job after work because he hadn't had one for a long time. We talked about because I wanted to know why I needed to do it as it seemed an odd request. The questions kept coming until in the end Drew just got short with me and me, and said I had to do it, or it was going to cause a problem for him. Work was horrible that day it was spent working but inside all I could do was dread what I knew I was going to have to do at the end of it so that nothing happened to Drew. In the little blue van on the way home Drew told the person he worked for who I thought was his friend as this had now become questionable. He was clearly an adult who Drew had known and been considered a family friend that must have actually been a no-good person. Now thinking back to it, it must have been these circumstances that caused Drew to distance himself from me because he felt bad. So, yeah, he told him I was going to do it and his friend pulled up somewhere out of sight so the deed could be done. I struggled to do it and Drew hid in the van I'm guessing so he didn't have to see it. In between trying to do what was asked of me I was heaving in between and was almost sick, so he stopped, but the weirdo was happy with the little I had managed to do, and we continued our journey home, him with a smile on his face and me and Drew in silence. I stopped going to the market after that. I have no idea why I was asked to do it and was unsure why Drew had gone from protecting me to getting me to do this. He had not only protected me every time we saw my dad, but he also took care of me and had stopped me completing an overdose. I knew I had upset him once by sleeping with someone else at the start of our relationship who turned out to be the boyfriend of someone I went to school with. We weren't friends but were in the same Math's class. She wanted to beat me up for it but one of her friends wouldn't let her, saying that she had no right to as she hadn't beat anyone else including any of her friends who had been with him behind her back knowing he was her boyfriend. But I never saw him again after that. Anyway, me and Drew became more distant, and we didn't have sex again until a new boy came to the home. He was a virgin and wanted to know what it was like to have sex so Drew suggested we do it with him to show him what it was like so, me him and Drew had a threesome. Shortly after that Drew moved out, I visited him in his place a few times but then it was like we never really knew each other.

I started to spend more time with a girl who used to live in the home who now had her own place, sometimes a lot of us would go there and sometimes it would be just me or a few of us. She always wanted someone with her, and we always wanted something to do so her place was the spot. We drank there, smoked there, ate food there, laughed there, argued there, did drugs there. In fact, it was there that I learned to roll a spliff which seemed quite odd considering how much I had grown up around it thanks to my dad and my aunt and their friends. My first roll was atrocious, so Selina suggested getting a packet of rizla and some toilet roll and practicing with that so I did, and it worked, and I have been able to roll perfectly ever since. Another resident, Shellie soon got her own place and sometimes we would go up there. But still spent most of our time at Selina's. Selina was a similar height to me with pale white skin and dark long curly brown bouncy hair that she wore in various styles some which maintained the curls and some that were with straight hair, and she had freckled cheeks. Things weren't always good here some of the arguments got out of control and she had men that would turn up when they felt like it and overtake her house. One of them was known for taking advantage of girls and making them do things being the new girl on the block I was next. He was just talking at first with his smarmy self in smarmy way and then looked me and said I looked like I could give good head. I refused to it at first and this panicked Selina. I saw from the corner of my eye the more the exchange of words continued the more worked up Selina was getting and so was the guy. I guess he was used to not having to go through this much to get his own way. He started to get closer to me and with that Selina told me to just go and do it or he was just gonna make me. He told me she was right. I got up and went in Selina's bedroom and sat on her bed. He stood right in front of me with his crutch opposite my face whilst he undid his belt and unzipped is black jeans and pulled out his erect self and shoved it in mouth. Bear in mind that I hadn't touched him in any way for him to even be aroused, which means he must have turned on by the situation. him I tensed up and got firm and he told me not make things worse for myself by biting him and grabbed hold of my hair tightly, so he had full control of my head. It didn't matter how much I heaved he kept going until he ejaculated. I was ready to throw up everywhere. He refused to let me move and told me I had to swallow otherwise he was gonna make me do it again. I feel like he must have been put in his place by someone at one point because he never came back well not that I remember anyway. I would see him sometimes driving around in his flash car, but he never said anything.

Another thing we could do in the home was earn money for doing the cleaning whoever was up first cleaned and got paid. They preferred if you stay home to do it but when me and Selina started doing speed, well I think she had done it before, but it was my first time. I would go to the home before the staff would wake up and clean so I could get paid when they woke and then go back to Selina's. Sometimes we would spend the money on food and other times it would be drugs or going out clubbing. I really enjoyed clubbing the atmosphere really drowned things out the pumping sound of your favourite music and the free release of the movement in your body when you dance.

Our group of girls soon became a mixed group as boys stared to come and chill and just chill, we would sit and talk, and nights would vary from deep conversations and late-night laughs. We got close to the boys and sometimes we would chill with them on our own or if someone in the mood they wouldn't come out in the car for a cruise or whatever. One of them in particular I got on with rather well and when we had a moment we slept together. I spent a few days back at the home and then had a message that Selina wanted to see me. Which seemed a strange request and no one knew why. I got ready and went round I knocked on the door and she jumped on me as soon as she opened it, punching me in the face in the head consistently one blow after another. I was still standing by the time she finished but confused as I didn't know what her problem was. A few months later when she apologised, I found out it was because she liked the guy I had slept with. But I didn't even know she liked him she never gave off that vibe and she never told me, and she was in relationships with other people and never with him.

It still didn't make sense though and what a shallow way to go about doing things. If I had known and done it anyway then yeah fair enough.

The circle soon came back together and new girl had joined, she was new to the home, and we took her under our wing. We soon regretted that when we all got ill with the same symptoms and had to take a trip to the STI clinic. There was three of us myself, Selina and Anna, the new girl we didn't have anything to hide from each other or so me and Selina thought. The nurse let us all come in together as we were friends and gave us all our results at the same time and then asked if we were all sleeping with the same person. We all looked at her I disgust and said no all pretty much at the same time. Baffled we took what we were prescribed for our Pelvic Inflammatory Disease (PID) which you get from having Chlamydia and Gonorrhea. No-one spoke on the way home and shortly after being back in the home Anna went to her room and me and Selina went back to hers and Selina came to the conclusion that Anna must have slept with the people who we were with at the time. We had been seeing our guys for a few months now and even Anna was in a relationship with one of the guys in the group. It transpired that she had cheated on her guy and slept with the guys that Selina and I were with.

Anna soon had her own place now so me and Selina went up there along with our friend Shellie. We had a go at Anna, so she knew we had realised what she had done and then beat her up whilst Shellie kept a lookout. Anna said she was sorry and asked if she could go in her kitchen and get a drink, we said of course she could, but she was taking ages to come back. Shellie went in the kitchen to see she wasn't there, and the front door was open. Selina suggested we leave as she must have gone to get help. We left and ran down the road a bit, so we were free from being near her area in case the police came, which they did. I was still running a bit when they stopped us but just said I was running to catch up with Shellie and Selina. They took our names and said they would be in touch if necessary. When I gave my name, the officer recognized the surname I was using at the time and asked if my dad was my dad, I said yeah and then the officer said isn't your dad doing some work in the community at centre. I didn't have a clue and I didn't know who he thought he was being out in the community like some nice guy as if he wasn't a woman beater and a pedophile. Anyone who suggests maybe he was trying to right his wrongs as he suddenly had a conscious, I will disagree with because I believe if he felt that bad, he could have at least told the truth to his family so that they wouldn't hate me anymore.

I just said to the officer that I wouldn't know because I was in a care home. Not being satisfied with calling the police Anna then reported us to the keyworkers at the home. Selina and Shellie were safe as they had their own places, I was the only still living in the home. The keyworkers sat me down and told me what had been said and asked if it was true. I admitted to my role and didn't say anything about anyone else. The keyworker said that she was surprised to hear what I had done especially as it was not that long ago that I was new myself so that I would know what it felt like to be in this position, I told them that, that is the exact reason why they should know I had good reason for my actions. Luckily, a place came up for me to live in and so was able to stay in the home until I got the keys, and I was moved straight in. Selina and Shellie were banned from visiting the home.

Not feeling wanted there and knowing my place was pretty much ready I picked up my duvet and started walking towards my flat. It was about 1 am and someone had seen me walking alone and offered me a lift. I hesitated at first, he said it was fine and it's just because I was late, and I was alone that he wanted to help. I hopped in the car, something I would never do now. But true to his word stopped the car when I needed him to, I got out, he drove off and I walked the rest of the way to where I needed to go, I spent the night on the floor in my living room.

Once the flat was sorted with carpet and secondhand furniture my flat became the new spot. Moving involved lots of filling out forms and applying for benefits as we no longer got allowances form the home or social services. A problem arose with my claim as they believed I was being fraudulent due to the spelling of my middle name. When I had gone to live with my dad, he had decided to change the spelling of my middle name as he had chosen it but hadn't like the way my mum had spelt it on my birth certificate. My outreach worker from the care home was able to rectify this for me. We had them for a while after moving out and they would come and do home visits, or we would meet for lunch.

The boys said they preferred it at mine because it was more chilled. Some of the girls I went to school with started to visit including my bully friend who was no longer bullying me. The crew grew and I would cook and some of them would come and eat, some to just chill and pass through. I was still with the guy I was seeing even after what happened with Anna. He pretty much moved in, and I thought we were exclusive until other people learned that I was with him and told me that he had a girl that he had been with for a long time. I had no clue and hadn't even heard of her and didn't know what to do. So, I did nothing. I had started going to college now and the guy I was with had a lovely yellow and blue Kappa jacket which I decided to where to college one day. That was the day I saw the girl for the first time. She didn't say anything to me but had obviously recognised the jacket. Later that evening the guy asked me if I wore his jacket to college, so something had obviously been said. A girl I knew from school, the same one who wouldn't let me get beat up at school for sleeping with the girl from school's boyfriend. Came to speak to me about the situation and I explained that I didn't knows about her to start with and that now I felt to involved to let go, but I would try to do the right thing. I told the girl about the STI incident so that the girl who was with the same guy as me could get checked as well and I learnt that this guy sleeping around was a regular so was no surprise when I woke with severe abdominal pain, so bad it was making me growl. Yep, you guessed it I had PID again. I was so devastated and overwhelmed I started to cut myself on my wrists with a razor blade. I was able to hide from others, but the guy noticed and told me I was a crazy bitch and that he didn't have time for these kind fuckeries. I didn't like what he said. The wounds stung as they healed which was annoying as it was like a constant reminder when you just wanted to forget you had done it. In the moment I done it, it helped as it was like releasing the pain through your skin.

We stopped sleeping together but him and all his boys would still come round and do their drugs. They had upped their drug game by this point and gone from just smoking weed and drinking to no now doing crack and Heroin. Some of the others had dropped off the scene a bit before this due to my front door being kicked off and my house being raided by armed police. As you can imagine the residents were not overly impressed whilst I feel bad for those in the community who were home, I was glad I wasn't as I have no idea what I would have done if I had of been in and had to face armed police.

Time had passed and I hadn't heard from him for a few days and the next time there was a knock at the door it was his mum. She had come to collect his things because he had gone to prison. I tried to go and visit him but was refused and then that was the end of it. Well so I thought.

He turned up again about a year later when I was in a new relationship and again when I was pregnant and tried to come in the bedroom whilst I was trying to put something decent on as I was just chilling with my new partner so wasn't fully dressed.

I made a friend in a neighbour who lived below me she turned out to be my little sister from my mum's side sister, they had the same dads. We got talking and started to spend time together and she became a great support, and she knew the people who used to come and chill in my flat. Selina never really came at the start but when they all stopped coming to me, I started to go back round to hers. It was always just me and her until she had to move out of her flat. Her mum offered for L to stay with her, Selina wasn't feeling too confident about this as their relationship was not great hence why Selina was where she was. Not having the close mother daughter relationship with my mum that I wished I'd have had I convinced Selina that this was a good step to take as it would help until she gets housed again and that a relationship with her mum may work better now. She did it and we both went to stay with her mum popping back to my flat every now and then.

We had run out of weed one night and Selina asked her mum if she had any idea of who we could go to. At first, she was like, how was she supposed to know as she didn't smoke herself. Then she was like actually the house over the road got raided a few weeks ago why not try over there. So, we did. And what a lovely surprise I got when the person who answered the door was someone I knew. It was the boy who I shared my first ever kiss with his name was Don. I remember it because his lips were soft and he held my face with his hand which was also soft, it gave me such a strange feeling and he was kind, his friends were messing about and banging stuff into the shed where we were sat. I got hurt and he shouted at them to stop and was making sure I was alright. I never saw him again after that because I had gone to live with my dad. And this boys' dad was my aunt's friend's boyfriend so that's I how I knew him as I would sometimes go there with my aunt. It was there that I had my second experience with drugs, my aunt told me to sniff this little bottle that she had. I sniffed it and got a headrush and then a headache. My aunt asked how I was feeling and so I told her, and she said see that's why you don't do drugs so don't do any.

Anyway, we look at each other and he said I know you don't I and I was like yeah, I think you do. We had a bit of chat and then me and Selina went back to her mums but still didn't have any weed. But his house soon became the spot which we almost lost when my mum was looking for me at their house and threatened them with the police if someone didn't tell her where I was. That obviously pissed off the dad and he said his piece to me, and I called my mum. I have no idea why she was looking for me and even though she stayed in touch on the odd occasion she left me in care and then moved to London and refused to let me go with her when I asked if I could come. That was the reason she was looking for me, so she could tell me she was moving. My mum came to the area in her white Ford Orion which she had, had for quite a while and she often fixed it herself using a car manual and even beat someone up on once. I was on my way home and hit the corner to see my mum going wild smashing some woman's head off the door frame of the car.

When she saw for herself, I was okay we had a chat and she warned be to be careful of L as she was more of a taker than a giver. I thought things would be good with us now so when she told me she was moving to London with my brother and sister I asked her if I could come, and she said no. I found it so upsetting and would just talk to people about it randomly but when people found out I was 17 they said she was right to leave me because I was old enough to fend myself now. Maybe that was true from their own experiences as I guess many had survived that situation themselves. But surely, they had struggles that could have been avoided or better for them if they had support. People seem to forget about that when others need support. The way I see it is just because you had to go through it, it doesn't mean that someone else should. That's the one thing that they may not be okay getting through. I also may have been ready legally, but I certainly wasn't emotionally.

I never knew why then and still don't know why now people use age to define if someone is ready for something. Your age only tells people how long you have been alive for it doesn't tell them your story and you may or may not be emotionally ready for what they think you should be ready for.

CHAPTER 9

More time was spent chilling with these guys and many others who came here, I had a connection that I recognise with the guy who I had shared my first kiss with and another guy in the room was more outspoken so we would flirt quite a lot. Little did I know he was only this way because he was on drugs and drinking all the time. He was a short stocky guy with well-defined body and a shaved head. He was very chatty and attentive large pupils and light brown eyes. If I'm honest with what I can see and know now I don't think I was ever really truly attracted to him. I guess it was more like an unconscious connection. The first time I asked him for a fag and asked him for one and he responded with

"Yeah, you can have anything you want."

He should have added that I could have anything I don't want too because I certainly got that. From that point onwards we always spoke, and he paid for me to come and see him at his friend's house in a taxi. He called Don's house and asked if I was there. Don's dad had answered and passed me the phone. After I said hello,

he said, "hello where are you?"

I replied "where am I? Well, you should know coz you just rang the house looking for me" we both laughed and so did everyone else in the room.

The taxi came and I went to the friend's house, and we all sat in his room. He had a bed that was an area that was sectioned off and after a few drinks and spliffs we kissed and had sex. After that we were together. I spent more time in my flat after that as I had him with me, and we would go and meet up with the others either at Don's house or in the parks in Woodley. It soon became apparent that my boyfriend was a pill head and used to take load at a time and sometimes would do acid tabs. I wasn't sure how I felt about this at first as I had had some drug experiences that hadn't gone too well. One of them was when I had some of what was called pink champagne which I was told was speed mixed with cocaine. I was already used to taking speed on the odd occasion and Selina told me I would be okay, so I took it. Whilst we were in the club, I kept getting these bouts of anger and Selina was telling me to chill out and to get control of myself because I wasn't really angry it was just the drugs. I think that night ended with having a go at a bar maid because my drink didn't taste like the one, I had ordered, which was Archers and Lemonade. Selina tasted it and said it was that and it didn't taste like to me because I had had so many.

The second unpleasant experience was when we were taking speed that we got from a new resident in the care home. This became the maddest experience I had had as I was starting to hallucinate and thought I could see a woman in a yellow coat putting her child in her red car. Selina said it was just the drugs and not worry. But when I laid down it felt like I had locked into the sofa and couldn't move, my body was floating even though it was still locked into the sofa. I was trying my best to get back into myself by trying to get of the lock so I could catch up with my body. I don't know how long this went on for but then our friend started collapsing, he would just lay there and then get up again and then just fall again like a log straight to the floor. Then he started vomiting, Selina started going mad telling him he had to clean it up, but he could hardly even move himself. The guy who sold us the speed turned up and Selina made him take our friend home. We later found he was in hospital because of his Sickle cell they ran tests on him to see what was affecting him in that way and they found Ketamine in his blood. So, our speed had been mixed with ketamine. Our friend recovered well.

My boyfriend decided to stop taking the pills, but he still drank and smoked and that's when the arguments started, I don't remember what it was about but I do remember slapping him in the face and so he said he was leaving. I had a meltdown and begged him not go I even got on the floor and grabbed hold of his ankles screaming and crying on the floor begging him not to leave me. He got out the door and came back. I didn't want him to go because he said he loved me, and he promised to always be kind to me and to protect me and to never let me get hurt again.

Things were calm again until we had our next argument, this time I hurt myself and smashed a wine bottle and used the glass to slice my wrists. He started to freak out was like oh my god what are you doing and took all the glass away from me. He was screaming I was screaming in pain; he was crying, and I was crying.

Things were calm again and we were still going to visit Don and the others and Selina had got quite close to them whilst I wasn't there and was helping when she could as Don had two younger siblings. Sometimes I didn't go and spent time with my friend downstairs. Where we got close our monthlies began to sync. One month we were both late and after checking with each other we calculated how many days late we were. But knowing this could happen sometimes we didn't think any more of it. She came on but I hadn't so she suggested getting a test which I did, and it came up positive. My dream had come true I was pregnant I was finally gonna have baby something I could love and that would love me back forever because I would give all the love, I never got. I wasn't worried about telling my boyfriend, even though he had said he didn't want to have kids. When I had got upstairs, he was stood on one foot in the bath and taking off his last sock ready to put his other foot into the bath. I waltzed in and said his name, entered the bathroom and then said, "I'm pregnant and I'm keeping it and if you don't like it then you can leave, and I'll do it by myself." I thought he was gonna leave as he said he didn't want kids but by this time he had also decided that he loved me more than his mum and it was no secret that I had wanted a baby and he was still happy to have sex with me.

My mum didn't want me to have a baby and had always said she was not gonna be nan for anybody. She warned me again on a call I had to her before I knew I was pregnant. Me and my boyfriend went to the phone box and called her, and we spoke to my mum and her sister. On that call my aunt had asked if I had any news. I didn't so I said no, she asked if I was sure, and I was.

My mum had seen a psychic who had told her that someone was going to be expecting. My mum and her sister knowing it wasn't them thought it was me. A week later I had to call back and tell them it was me and explain that I hadn't known at the time I asked.

When they accepted that I was keeping the baby I got a letter from my mum saying that I shouldn't have a baby as I wasn't ready and that it wasn't going to be easy and who did I think would help me when I needed it because she wouldn't.

Levi used to come and visit with his wife, and I showed them the letter. He said he wasn't surprised and that I shouldn't have anything to with my mum because she just wasn't worth it and had no place to say what she was saying as she couldn't even look after me. My aunt came round with her boyfriend, and I showed her the letter which I later couldn't find so she had obviously taken it.

After years of being slim and being able to wear whatever, I wanted, sometimes not leaving much to the imagination. I began to put on a lot of weight and very quickly as well going out became difficult mentally and physically with the difficulties I was beginning to have with sciatica. I still went out when I could and when I wasn't out, I spent days sleeping. Soon I started staying in altogether after hearing people talking about me and how fat I had got. First it was some girls we hung around with in Woodley. We were walking to the park from a friend's house, and I could hear them saying how they were never gonna have a baby because they didn't want to be fat like that and were laughing at the clothes I was now wearing. The other time was at a party we had organised it was good loads of people came, we made money on the door and the music was good. Even though I was pregnant I had a good dance but towards the end of the night to my favourite song at the time, which was Rewind by Craig David, I was tired and sat down to chill. A couple next to me were talking about having sex and I heard the guy say to the girl let's make sure we take precautions coz I'm sure you don't want to end up like that, look at her. Which is a good thing in a way especially if they knew that wasn't right for them but at the time it made me feel shit. And little did they know it was my past life dragging me down and had me looking like that not being pregnant.

Labour started in the middle of the night first I was being sick over the toilet and then I felt something pop and then water splatted on the floor. We called the hospital and they told us to come in, so we called a taxi. It took like ages for us to get down the stairs in between contractions as they were coming thick and fast, but we eventually made it. The taxi driver wasn't impressed and said if anything happened in his car, we would have to pay for it.

We got there and I was hardly dilated, and it turned out that only my back waters had broken, they said they usually send people home when it's like this but because of how much pain I was in so early on they decided to keep me in. It had also recently been noted that I had high blood pressure, so they had concerns over possible pre-eclampsia so bang went my idea of a home birth.

They hooked me to up monitors to keep an eye on me and the baby. They later moved me to a ward and gave my boyfriend a chair so he could sit at my bedside. He was okay with this until I turned to face the other way not to be away from him but because it was more comfortable this way well as comfortable as you can get in labour. I didn't know he had taken offence to this until he was like "fuck you then I'm going for a fag." I asked why he was being like this, and he said,

spread your wings, speak your truth, write it down & let it 96 go

"well may as well not be here you're not even looking me you're just facing the other way." I explained why and he was like oh well okay I'm still going for a fag, and I'll be back. Early hours in the morning a midwife gave me some pethidine and I was soon zoning in and out and wasn't able to worry about what he was saying or doing.

I remember being checked and I was 8cms dilated so they moved me to the labour suite. I wasn't comfortable on a bed, so my boyfriend basically held me up for the duration of it, when I met him, he was a hod carrier and a brick layer, so he had the arms for it. He had his arms under my armpits whilst I crouched down dragging us both down in the moments of pain. Labour had gone on for a while and they couldn't get a clear trace of the baby's heartbeat, so they tried the next best thing and that was putting a clip on the baby's head. Which ended up with the midwives in fits of laughter. Not what you want to hear when your legs are sprawled open and people looking up there. When the midwife saw the look on my face, she confirmed that she was not in fact laughing at me but at the fact that they were trying to put a clip on the baby's head, but it kept popping off and flying back out of me because of the amount of hair she had.

My daughter started to make her way out and all I could feel was a whole heap of pressure and burning inside my vagina. As she came out, I could feel her hair and then out came her legs with another gush of water and blood. I got a glimpse of this blue body and black hair. I did what felt like pass out. The door to the room we were in flew open and all these white coats come flying in and then my boyfriend started screaming "oh my god what's happened to my baby?" When I came back round, I asked what was going on. Then we heard her cry. We don't know what happened as to why she was born blue, but we were glad she was alive. I wasn't sure if it was connected but I remember having to go to the hospital because I stopped feeling her move as much. I was told all was fine as long as I counted 10 movements in day. I was able to do that, and she was more active on weekends and that's how things were when she was born, chilled in the week and lively on the weekends. She was born at 12:38 on a Saturday afternoon, weighing 7lb 5oz. We were kept in for a few days because of the complications and my blood pressure.

Whilst I was there my older sister came to see me, I wasn't expecting her she swished back the curtain of the bed I was in and was stood there with another girl who I didn't know. Congratulations she says like it's normal barging into someone's hospital curtain unexpectedly. She tells me who her friend is, so I say hi and she said hi back and then my sister asks what I had and then amongst the small talk she says, "so when you gonna let dad see her then?" There it was a dirty mark on a good space. I told her straight that I'm not why would I after what he has done to me. The conversation came to a holt, and she left. I knew that wasn't the end though because her boyfriend was friends with my neighbour's boyfriend and so they had started to talk.

My aunt came to see me which was yet another altercation as she had come with my cousin and other children are not allowed in the hospital when you have a new baby unless they are the baby's siblings. After explaining that they had travelled all the way from Luton and that she was the only family we had they were allowed in. We were quite close then and when I lived with my mum, we spent quite a bit of time there and I stayed quite a lot. One time she had planned to run away with me and her boyfriend who would soon become her husband.

When I was finally allowed home after a heated discussion with a midwife as apparently, I couldn't go home yet anyway because I'd had a C- section which I hadn't. When I said that she asked what kind of birth did you have then? Well, that was a bit concerning to me with her being the midwife surely, she should know it was a vaginal delivery if it wasn't a C-section. She checked my notes and saw I was right and said she was sorry as she was running late this morning and missed some of the handover. Which to me meant she wasn't in a position to be arguing. There was still some concern over my blood pressure, but I argued that surely it would go down better at home because I wasn't comfortable or happy in the hospital. It was agreed but I had to call the hospital if anything changed. Finally, I was home and then after a few days my aunts' friend drove us to Luton, and I had my midwife care transferred to there. My aunt spent hours on the phone with my mum trying to get mum to come over. She didn't want to but did in the end with my little sister who showed a great interest in my daughter, my mum didn't though she just looked at her. Whilst we were there me and my boyfriend had our first disagreement about our daughter. I wanted to cream her skin after she had a bath, but he didn't want me to. I said it needed doing so I was going to do it, but my aunt stepped in and said she was his baby too, so I had to let him have his say. Three days later I was absolutely horrified when I took off my daughter's baby grow to see her skin all white and flaky where she had been being bathed and not moisturised. As people who were raised to cream our skin, I surprised to see my aunt didn't think it was necessary. That day I creamed her skin and did so every day after that, but I don't feel her skin was the same again.

I started to pass huge clots and so my aunt called the midwife out but even though they were quite large they weren't coming frequently enough for them to be concerned. My aunt showed me how to hand express and we tasted my milk from a mug, the only thing I've ever had since that I feel even comes close is rice milk.

My aunt wasn't best pleased though when her boyfriend cooked, and I didn't eat it all. I only left some tinned tomatoes and that was because the acid in the tomatoes was not agreeing with me. I tried explaining I think where I had the baby... she cut me off right there and said that was no excuse, but she didn't even know what I was gonna say. I didn't have the energy to answer back I was feeling sick, and it been over week since I last had any bowel movement so that couldn't have helped. Her boyfriend was okay about it though and took my plate anyway.

When it was time to go home, we cried and had to be pried from each other's arms and I cried all the way back in to Reading in her other close friend's car.

We adjusted to parenthood and my boyfriend got a job in Reading as a plasterer which made more sense as he had moved in now and was glad to get away from his other job as he wasn't happy with some of the things, they said to him when they found out I was black. Asking him things like if he took me bananas home instead of flowers.

I enjoyed being a new mum and my baby slept well so that helped, we still went to Don's house and chilled in Woodley and everyone enjoyed seeing our little girl. When she was 8 months old, I was starting feel the stress as I was having trouble moving her from breast to bottle. And my boyfriend's grandad was dying so he was also stressed. I went with him to see his grandad and the rest of his family. I had a moment with him in the room, but my boyfriend had a go at me saying that he is not a thing to looked and stared so I left. Being a person who is in interested in people and how they are I was just trying to get a feel for him as a person and felt it was so sad. I didn't think any more of it as it was a grim time.

I bumped into a woman called Janine who used to be friends with my mum, she was of dual heritage and had broad shoulders and got smaller as she went down. She was easy to talk to and a good comforter, I knew this from when she comforted me the first time, I had spoken out about being raped. They went to school together, but they fell out in Christmas 1998 at my mum's house in London. We were all invited up for Christmas and we all had to bring food to share. Everything was going well until my mum's friend Janine wanted to go and spend the night with a male friend that she had got to know through my mum he lived round the corner from her, and Janine wanted to leave her daughter with us. But my mum wasn't having any of it this time as she felt it was a regular thing and had, had enough of being taken advantage of. When my mum moved to London, she went without telling Janine and had hoped to keep the distance. They argued and Janine left, and I think she took her daughter with her.

This all happened the same year I met my boyfriend, we had been together just over a month, so he came with me.

So anyway, I bumped into her in town, and we had a chat and she stayed in touch and started coming round to my flat and I started going

spread your wings, speak your truth, write it down & let it 100 go

to hers as time went on it was though she had become the perfect mother figure. She started to have our daughter overnight which gave me time to myself and time for us to go out which was pointless really as it always ended up in an argument. One date night we went out to slough, and I don't even remember what triggered the argument, but he got so nasty and I spiteful, you could see the spite in his face and hear the bitterness in his words I ended up by myself crying at the train station and had to go back home alone on the train. I called Janine for help but all she could do was advise as she had our daughter. I made it back into Reading safely and went back to my flat. He turned up the next day all sorry saying he didn't know what had got into him and that it wouldn't happen again. If only I had of known how many times, I was going to hear that over the 14 years that we were together. It did happen again one night we were at Janine's an argument started and it continued until we got home where he pulled a knife on me and me gripped up against the door and held a knife to my throat. All I could feel was the cold sharpness of the blade of knife pressed against my neck scared to even swallow. He dropped the knife and proceeded to strangle me with both his hands gripped tightly around my neck. Our daughter was in the next room, I don't what made him let go but he did thankfully. This time I felt fear as no matter how much I struggled or tried to hit back nothing made a difference. It was mad weird as we seemed so connected and he noticed important things. Like me not being present during sex he said it felt as though I wasn't there or like I wasn't interested. He was right I wasn't there I had learnt to disassociate during sex. I consciously tried to be more conscious apart from the nights we were high as it didn't matter then.

We were in a good phase when my nan came over from Grenada to visit, but I started to see a different side to my nan then. She was her usual self in terms of always buying things and stocking up on things, cracking jokes and going out to socialise. She always got nice things and spotted bargains and it was nice to have some food cooked by her hands. But she would talk down to me a lot and could never just say anything without being extreme about it. Like "take the child's dummy out of your mouth before you give the baby cancer" and then she would moan about it for ages. Another time she saw me taking me pill and said, "oh my gosh you gotta have sex so much." I get she didn't get that I had to take it every day anyway not just when you have sex.

We slept in the living room on a sofa bed whilst she was here and one morning she walked in and there was no cover on my boyfriend, so she saw him naked and was horrified. I heard saying to herself in her Caribbean accent "oh god him sleep naked". The same morning, I heard her calling me a nasty little bitch all because I had left a few side plates in the sink from the night before.

One funny night we had my nan said she was going out for dinner with her friend so we asked Selina if her and boyfriend could babysit so we could have a bit of break for a few hours. They came round to get our daughter, but we decided to have a spliff together before they went. A few tokes in we heard a key in the door my boyfriend grabbed everyone's joints jumped into the kitchen and on to the kitchen sink and opened the Velux window and rested the spliffs on the roof. We all sat quietly and said hello to her as she came in. I said, "I thought you was going out for dinner" she said, "I did I went out and eat and come back." We let some time pass and then when we found a good moment my boyfriend gave Selina and her boyfriend back their spliffs and they left. My nan came and sat with as and watched TV her nose started twitching and she said that something smelt funny. I looked at her and had to think quick, the kitchen was next to the living room and from where I was sitting the cooker was in my line of site. So quickly said I was frying something not long before she came in., she told me in future I needed to open the window when I am frying things.

I got back in to smoking and drinking once I had stopped breast feeding as I had stopped once I found out I was pregnant. This continued until I found myself drunk quicker than usual after drinking cans of special brew and was struggling to smoke even a cigarette. In the end I decided to do a pregnancy test but wasn't expecting the results to be what they were as I was taking my pill and hadn't missed any. My boyfriend wasn't happy as he didn't even want to have any kids in the first place. He came from a big family he had 7 siblings and at one point they all lived together until one of his brothers left. When I first went to stay, we had to share a room with his siblings. For me it was nice to be in a household where everyone was together and getting along. I was looking forward to being part of unit. We had a bit of a rocky start as my boyfriend had an STI to begin with and they felt that I had given it to him. But I felt he had given it to me because the first time we got intimate he seemed to have an unusual amount of sticky discharge that he was unable to explain. We both took medication and never had the problem again.

I made it very clear that I was not going to have an abortion, that just wasn't for me, and this conversation triggered what happened when I first moved in with my dad this time, I got more books that showed more detail about pregnancy and its stages and the fetus sizes. When I went to the midwife appointment, I talked about it with her as she was unable to find the heartbeat of this baby even though my test was positive. I had to stay in the hospital for an extra day and thankfully everything was fine. But the initial appointment where she was having trouble locating the heartbeat, this triggered the conversation about what I found in the seat of knickers the morning after I was in pain at my dad's. She confirmed that I had in fact had a miscarriage. I was speechless in that moment I had learned that I had flushed a baby down the toilet. How awful!

This time my weight was steady but there was something about this pregnancy that made me know I was having a boy. I was all set buying the clothes when I bumped into my older sister who seemed like she took great pleasure in talking me out of buying them because there was no way I could know I was having a boy. But I don't know how I knew that I knew but I did. Six months in and my weight blew up again and my sciatica was worse this time round and so it was more difficult to walk. Having another argument during this time also didn't help and this time he completely battered me he punched me, pushed me, kicked me, and even stamped on me whilst I was on the floor. Our little girl was two then and by this point she had heard quite a few things and had experienced quite an abrupt and angry attitude from me one time when it came to tidying up her toys. But my little old neighbour from the flat across the way plucked up the courage to say his piece to me and told me I shouldn't have kids if that's how I was going to be and then he ran out. That hit a nerve and cut deep but, in that moment, he was right as in certain moments I was not coping well but I knew I loved my daughter and knew I had to change that part about me, so I did. But this obviously wasn't enough to protect her from her everything. And in this moment, I couldn't do anything to help her as she screamed from the distress she was hearing and feeling whilst she listened to me screaming with every blow I received whilst I was curled up against the bedroom wall in between the door and the wardrobe taking everything he did, too scared to move in case he caught my pregnant belly. I don't remember what the argument was about, but I called his mum to try and help diffuse it, but this didn't stop him through the phone. In fact, it was after this that he started going for it and even his mum was screaming at him to stop. That day she heard her son become an animal and have complete disregard to what was going on around him and what he was doing. My daughter screamed so much that in the end she just stopped. When he had decided to stop, he left, and I crawled to into the living room to go and sit with my daughter. All I could do was hold her and we both just sat there and didn't speak, and she continued to not speak for two weeks. I didn't know what to do and tried to just keep being mum. Taking her out going to the shops, to the park buying sweets. Janine and her daughter came round the next day and saw the bruises I had they were blacker than my skin. This day we were supposed to go to his mate's house, but he asked if I could stay home as he didn't want Don or his dad to see what he had done. I agreed to stay home because I didn't want any of them to see me like that. Janine told me that I needed to get away from him. But I didn't know how, and he said he was sorry and that it wouldn't happen again, and it only happened like that because he thought it was gonna be the last time because he thought our relationship was gonna be over.

Drew from the care home came to Reading to visit my boyfriend wasn't happy about this but I didn't know he was coming he just turned up. Before he left, he told me he was going to be at the care home the next day and so if I wanted to see him then to go there as he would be waiting. If I wasn't there by a certain time then he would be gone and that would be it, I went out that day and I did consider going to the home, but I think I overthought it and didn't go as I was thinking what if he wanted us to be together again, it wouldn't fair to keep my daughter from her dad. Especially as I would have been doing the one thing I was trying to avoid and that was creating a broken family unit. Effectively that is what was happening anyway, but I couldn't see that at the time. But after often wondered what life would have had in store for me if I did go. My boyfriend thought that I was going to go and as soon as I got back, he asked me if I went, he was relieved. It didn't help though that I had an ex turn up before this he just turned up and waded his way in and said he wanted to try on some clothes. I told him he couldn't and had to get as my boyfriend was coming over, which I should never have said as he took this as a cue to create a problem and tried his clothes on anyway. Being slow to do it so as my boyfriend arrived, he was just finishing putting his top back on, so it looked like we had been up to something.

The following week I went to Don's house, his dad always gave me advice and told me that he always knew that I was never lying about the rapes. But on this day as I walked in, he said "well I'll tell you what your first mistake was and that was not getting with my son." I surprised to hear that, but I knew he was right, and I told him that. I said "well I know that now but what can I do about it when I've gone and had a kid with his friend and if I do anything now it will cause problems within the friendship group. The conversation was left at that.

Sometimes Don's dad would drive us home after visiting I was always grateful for the lift and this night it was a good job; we did get one because that was the night I went into labour. My boyfriend's cousin had predicted that this was going to happen he was like "ooh my gosh look at the size of that bump there's no way she can get any bigger than that."

During Labour I was in so much pain, obviously. I had pethidine in the fridge but was trying to go as long as possible without it. I was at home this time so was a lot more comfortable as I could be than if I was in the

spread your wings, speak your truth, write it down & let it 105 go

hospital. As the pain grew more intense, I started growling that this was his fault. The midwife thought that the person I was moaning about was the father, but my boyfriend explained it was because his cousin had said it was going to happen today and it did. Rather than just breaking one time my waters kept on popping in various places. In the midwife decided to burst them with the hook they use to try and speed things along. They soon figured out that the baby's back was against my back another last-minute shock. He had created one 2 weeks before I went into labour as he had grown an extra 2 CMS which was unusual, so close to the due date. Janine and her now teenage daughter had taken my daughter on a little seaside holiday. So, she wasn't there when this happened it was also the morning of my aunts wedding, she had wanted us to go up so we could be there for the wedding and said not to worry about going into labour as I could have the baby there, but I didn't want to do that, and we couldn't afford to do that. What a good job I didn't as I would have been stuck in the hospital instead of at the wedding. I feel like she was only making a big thing of it to try and make up for never wanting to have me as her bridesmaid. Me being would have been like she had been invisibly forgiven because it would have meant that I was accepting of it so she could be married free of that guilt. It seems like a deep insight to a minor thing but that was important to me and ever since I was a child, she had always promised that I would be her bridesmaid when she got married.

The midwife could see he was not turning so she went in for the kill and stuck her arm up me and spun the baby round by his head and he was soon born. She put him on my belly, and I was in shock, if I hadn't of been there for the birth, I would have sworn they had given me the wrong baby because of how white he was, especially against the blackness of my skin. He was a lovely 8lb 10oz, born at 6:30am on a Saturday morning. It was so nice to relax after in the comfort of my own bed and being at home meant I could have whoever I wanted to visit. He was born crying and then cried what seemed like every half an hour after that. It seemed like he was always feeding and was never settled.

I have since then learnt that if you have depression and other mental health issues during pregnancy those can affect your unborn child as these circumstances influence the hormones and chemicals that you carry around your body. Then once the fetus reaches a certain stage of the pregnancy, they can hear what goes on around them. So, this means that he not only felt my distress whilst I was carrying him, but he could also hear what was going on. I was also having therapy for the rapes. I had gone to the doctors about getting help as my boyfriend kept on telling me that I was crazy and needed help. My appointments just happened to come up when I was pregnant.

Things with me and my boyfriend were not getting any better and became more than just violence, he would be verbally and emotionally abusive telling me I was ugly and useless and dirty and was always accusing me of cheating on him. It was all hurtful, but nothing hurt more than the day he told me I deserved to be raped. We were already arguing when Selina and her boyfriend came over, so they kept hold of our daughter whilst it was happening. I was doing my best ignore him by doing the hoovering and it was going well until I heard "look at you, you're nothing, ha, you deserved to get raped and knowing you, you probably enjoyed it." That was it for once I had lost it, and with the hoover still on I lashed him with the hoover pole I heard L shout no Nyasher don't, but it was too late I was already in full swing hitting him. He thought he was funny to begin with because he had an audience even though they weren't encouraging him he still felt empowered by them. A few times they told him to stop and told him he was out of order, but he just carried on. In the moment I hit him he just stood there and did nothing.

In the end I did feel useless and worthless and like nothing.

CHAPTER 10

We soon moved from the flat to a two bedroomed upside-down house, I call it this because when you went in the house the kitchen was on the right and the living room round a tiny corner to the left next to the top of the stairs and the bedrooms, bathroom and toilet were downstairs. The place was grubby and dirty, the council said they would send someone round to do a clean before we moved in, but they never did, and we had an infestation of German cockroaches. I already struggled with housework as it was because of a mixture of depressions and ill physical health and it seeming like that was all ever did. I came to realise that I had been a mum for longer than the day I had my first child. When I lived with my mum, I did the school drop off and pick up, I had the after-schoolteacher conversations, I made the meals and did the housework and anytime my mum agreed to babysit I was one who did the looking after. I didn't have to do the school drop or looking after when I lived with my dad, but I did have to sometimes go shopping, I remember being seen by my bully friend and she said to me that I look like an old haggard woman in her 40s run down with kids. And you know what that was exactly how I felt. But now I am 40 that is most definitely not how I feel. Other than my fibromyalgia I actually feel younger and freer than I did then and have ever done.

My boyfriend didn't really help much so I still kind of felt like I was on my own but at the same time I was overly independent. This is a trauma response but also not helped by people constantly letting you down but it's hard to attract the right kind of people of you are not right in yourself. When I did ask him to do things, he never did it when it needed doing, never being sure if he would just actually ever get round to it, I would just get on with it in the end. I did sometimes think he would just leave it knowing I would do it myself in the end anyway. When I first started to this, it was though he felt emasculated as it was like he was deflated and then he would say why did you do that I was going to do it. But there is only so long you can wait for things to be especially when people don't expect you to get them done as well. The housing officer I was given didn't think we would get the place sorted but when he came and saw it was done, he was impressed and even took on of our room ideas to use elsewhere. We had painted the hallway terracotta and white and that was what he had liked.

Tessa had a christening for her baby we were invited as a family, but my boyfriend didn't want to go he chose to stay home and kept our daughter with him, and I took our son who was still a baby. As I walked in there was a mixture of people who I did didn't know. One guy said a little bit louder than I think he anticipated "ooh who's that?" We were introduced to each other and ended up getting on well and I started to feel good. We went off on our own and talked and laughed some more until one thing led to another, we had sex. My son was sleeping in his pushchair and was with Tessa and her friends and family. I felt so guilty after that I left and went home and when I got home, I was sick and couldn't stop throwing up. I tried to be as normal as I could around him, but I struggled, I didn't go near him or let him near me. By the second day of this I was so overwhelmed, and guilt ridden that I left. I waited for him to go to work packed up mine and the kids' things wrote a note telling him what I had done and left. I went to stay with Tessa and kept my daughter off nursery so he couldn't find me, for fear of getting beaten up. He figured out where I was, and spray painted a message on the floor saying our love was one in a million. He had to be sure I was there to do that so I'm guessing he partially did what he used to do when he would go off on one after starting an argument which was to hide out and spy.

But with the arguments as he would say he was going to kill himself and then go out. I would end up going to look for him to make sure he didn't. I never knew he was hiding out and watching me, until one day he said that I didn't look hard enough because he could see me so why couldn't see him. Once I knew he was watching me I stopped looking for him when he went off. I wasn't playing games I thought he was serious I would never have left our daughter with anyone otherwise. It was so infuriating as I would go and look for him out of worry or fear or both him sometimes it was so dark where it was so late and so when we had our I'd have to leave my daughter with someone whilst I went to look, down dark alley ways and car parks. I feared something happening for me to and then the fear of having to go back and find something had happened to my daughter would make me stop and go back home.

I stopped staying with Tessa after that and went to stay with Janine and I was now spending more time with the guy I had cheated with. My boyfriend was now my ex knew this and then started saying he wanted to see the kids which I let him do but the day he came I had a pregnancy testing kit in a bag I had, and he saw it and was like oh I see how it is now. I told him it wasn't like that it was just to check as I was taking contraception.

He had a bit of cheek trying to be upset about it though. Before I stopped having to stay Tessa's my friend Marissa came to visit me at Tessa's and then went back and told Warren, the father of my kids that I got sexy Underwear. I had brought underwear, but it wasn't sexy it was just to wear. But he took boundless joy in throwing that in my face and didn't stop think that it was weird that she was taking things back to him. It's not like she was someone who lived by morals when it came to things like this. She had cheated on her long-term boyfriend pretty much throughout their relationship with various boys from school. It soon came to light that she had even been with more than I knew about. I wasn't in the right headspace to put things together then, but he was always happy for her to come round. During one of my domestic incidents, she was on the phone whilst he was hitting me, I asked her to call the police for me, but she said she couldn't and just sat on the phone and listened. It soon transpired that the reason for the information being taken back to Warren, was that they were sleeping together my best friend of 10 years was sleeping with the father of my kids. There had to be more to this than just sex because she had already slept with him twice when we had a threesome for his birthday and then again, a week later. The first time we all got a kick out of out and mine my boyfriend's sex life really got a boost. We decided to try it again, but it wasn't the same this time round. Everyone knew we were going to do it and then everyone knew we had done it and was excited and curious about it. So, we talked about it a lot.

Whilst Marissa was sleeping with the father of my kids, I was seeing the guy I had cheated with, so I wasn't mad that Warren was sleeping with someone else it was more about who he was sleeping with. My aunt's friend who had now become my friend said to me I had no right to be mad because she basically had permission from when I first invited her into my bed. But I didn't agree to this and felt that this was different as this was behind my back and Marissa as my friend should have been upfront with me.

There's a lot to be said about watching how people treat others around them because if that's how they can treat those who they say they love or are naturally supposed to love then it makes sense they would do something to you or in some way or another. Obviously not everyone is like and this and do just treat others accordingly. She avoided me for ages, but we bumped into each other in town and arranged to go on a night out at the Face bar. I could see she was uneasy but played the role of her friend and acted like I knew nothing about her and the father of my kids. We went to the bar and had a drink together and then was dancing together. I told her my feet were hurting and she offered to swap boots because she liked mine. I agreed and said we would meet back in the toilets at the end of the night to swap back before going home. When that time of night came that's exactly what we did, and I also took that moment to confront her about what had been going on with her and Warren.

"Oh, so he told you then" she said looking unimpressed.

"Of course, he told me I said I don't know what made you think he wouldn't, you're not special I have his kids not you. And don't think you'll be seeing him again because you won't be we're getting back together."

"Oh, are you she" said sheepishly "but I thought" she continued

"You thought what?" I said because whatever it was you were thinking ain't happening because who do you think has got the kids now so I could come out in the first place.

The colour drained from her face and I lost it and hit her in the face with her boots and took mine back, her sister was angry and wanted to fight me, but she knew Marissa was in the wrong.

I had stopped seeing the guy I had been cheating with but was still staying with Janine. Janine had been popping back to the house to check on things and get clean things for me and the kids. She caught Marissa there once so I think that might even be why Warren came clean. After that Warren started to do the house up and actually lay the laminate flooring we had, I had been waiting for him to lay for ages. Janine and her daughter started telling me how nice the house was without me there and how it was so much tidier. Nice huh. I had to point out that obviously it would be when it's just him there and no kids to clean up after. And remind them of how long we had, had the laminate for and he was only just putting it down now.

I didn't see Marissa again after that until she came to my house a few months later to tell me that she was pregnant, and she thought it was Warren's. She came to me to see what she should do. Warren was now my boyfriend again after a lengthy talk about things that had to change. We talked about building our family up and having more children and getting married and how things weren't going be how they used to be then I moved back in. He was on a job round the corner, so I left Marissa with my kids and went round there to tell him. He said he wasn't interested as he didn't want a baby with her. This finalised her decision as her boyfriend who she had been with since school had already told her to get rid of the baby because there was no way he was going to walk the streets with her with a baby that people would suspect was Warren's. And so that's what she did, even though she didn't want to have an abortion again. The last time I saw her after that was in town she was with a different man, and I couldn't help myself when I saw her and just shouted out "oi Marissa whose man have you teef now?" She just looked at me with embarrassment and looked away. Her man looked at me too but didn't say anything. Nothing more was said but I knew that if she hadn't already told him what had gone on then she was going to have some explaining to do. Unless he wasn't bothered by it. I Haven't seen her again since. But I have heard that she married him and had another child.

Life started to change Tessa went on holiday for a while, Warren went to get some help for his anger and drinking and had some therapy sessions well about three and was given antidepressants, which he only took for a short amount of time because he said he felt better so didn't need them anymore. We had another baby and got engaged. Things seemed fine and his glazing job was going well, and they even paid for his driving lessons, and he passed his test. Using some money from the compensation my mum was awarded from a fall in a supermarket before she died and some money from my step aunty, we got a people carrier with a sliding door.

My mum died the same year my third child was born. She had been diagnosed with Motor Neurons Disease, no one knew how or why as it was not something to our knowledge that was in our family line. My brother told me about her diagnosis and what had happened. She just collapsed in the garden one afternoon and no one knew why and then she had a fall in the supermarket which seemed to make it worse. We were even more estranged at this point as she hadn't really been there for me, and my brother had moved out because of how she was towards him, and other people were quick to interfere by criticising and not advising and supporting.

I guess they thought they were better than her because they still had their kids living with them, but they just like my mum also had sordid pasts and were not perfect and now of age their children have grown up to make choices they are not happy with.

My mum got weaker as time went on and as the illness got worse, first her knees went, then her legs, her hands, her arms in the end she was in a wheelchair and had to be bathed and fed. Some days I felt bad for her and other days I wondered if this was her karma for not being a good mum to me. My nan was said she was upset with how things had got between us as she knew I would have helped to take diligent care of her. My brother took care of her, he had stayed in touch when he left and as soon as he knew she was sick he was there by her side every week without fail. My brother had seen that those who were quick to encourage him to leave his mum weren't there for but our mum who had been painted in a bad light was still reaching out to him. I know at times he found it difficult, not just because she was his mum but also because she was very independent regardless of whether she was in a relationship or not. She was always so private and kept things separate. It looked like she had gone from this tower of strength to just a ball of vulnerability. As she now needed to be pushed around and lifted, fed, and bathed. but she was still strong and did her best to fight every day and could still move her legs and feet a little even though they said she wouldn't be able to.

On the days, my brother wasn't there she had carers in, but some stole things from her, and some didn't have a clue what there were doing. Because a lot them whilst washing her would use the same water to wash her face after they had already washed her other parts, she wanted them to use Dettol in the water to help her feel cleaner. When she asked one of the ladies to do that, the lady put Lenor fabric softener in it instead. At one point she tried out a care home, she went in on her time of the month which she made known, and they just left her in her sanitary towel for a lot longer than they should have and she had to wait three days for a bath.

My mum reached out to me and started to open up about some things one of them was that she was sorry she wasn't able to protect to me from what happened to me as she never wanted that for me, but she was in a difficult position. Because Ashbert was always after their mum's money and my mum had all the paperwork that she was trying to keep safe. So, some of the time she was out she was out because she was moving it. She also said she knows that isn't a good enough excuse, but she doesn't have any other way to explain. It was an emotional moment that was held with silence. We then went on to talk about her illness as she knew she was going to do die and she said she had known all along but she didn't want anyone around her who was going to be there out of pity. Then she asked if she could see me which I agreed to and then she asked me to bring the baby. I had had my third child by then, he was also born at home. Towards the end of the pregnancy, I ended up housebound because of Symphysis Pubis dysfunction. This is when you get discomfort in your pelvic region and your joints come out of place and move unevenly or become stiff, usually this only occurs during pregnancy. On the day I went into labour I was trying to make plans to go town as I was feeling energised, good job I couldn't find anyone to go with, shortly after I found myself experiencing contractions. I called the midwife and two of them came out in good time. My contractions slowed down so they continued their home visits. I called Warren, and he came home but we struggled to get hold of the midwives when things became intense again. Warren looked to see if he could see what was going on but said he couldn't see anything. The midwives soon returned with gas and air. I did try a TENS machine which helped at the very beginning but then it just became annoying, so I took it off. I soon relinquished the Gas and Air as it made me vomit and for some reason it was pink. Janine's daughter came as well, we were always close from when my mum and Janine were friends, and we found our bond again from when I bumped into Janine in town. Janine was away at this time due to whatever she had going on, so I did my best to look out for Aimee her daughter. soon my bedroom was full, there was myself, Warren, 2 midwives and Aimee until things seemed like they were going wrong. The paramedics were called and four of them came. My son soon arrived into the world, still inside his sac which had to be broken from around him when he came out. He came out, weighing 9lb 13oz at ten past four in the afternoon. Having not had any pain relief I was feeling a bit self-conscious about having all those people around me, mainly because I had learnt that midwives can see if you have had any vaginal scarring so can generally tell if you have been raped. Knowing that I had vaginal scarring meant I knew they could see what had happened to me, I even tried to close my legs and had to be told to open them again as they were waiting for the afterbirth to come out. They made some jokey bets about how much the afterbirth was going to weigh. No one got it right as surprisingly it almost weighed the same amount as the baby. The paramedics ended up not being needed but they were happy they had attended as it was the first time, they had witnessed a birth. They thanked me for the experience. The midwives ran me a lukewarm bath and Warren helped me get in and kept an eye on me and helped me get out. The midwives tidied up the bedroom and waited for me to get settled back in bed, they wanted to some checks on the baby before they went but we couldn't find him it was as though he was actually missing but he was with Aimee, she had taken him upstairs. Things were different with this this baby as he was always content, and I found it difficult to mother him as he was happy to not be in hands all the time. When he could crawl, he would go off and sit in random places like under the table and behind the door, his favourite place was in the toy box under the window. I think it was because you could see the river and the ducks and people going by.

I spoke to Janine on the phone and told her what had happened, and she said to me that it was up to me if I wanted to go and see my mum, but she didn't think I should but if I took the baby with me then she wouldn't be happy and would never speak to me or help me again. That confused me even more and I felt stuck. What was I to do take risk and lose help knowing that my mum wouldn't even be able to help me anyway as she was going to die and so lose the help either way? Or keep the help from Janine which I felt like I needed and upset my mum by not bringing my baby.

I went without him and was conflicted the whole time, when we me and my brother arrived, I felt glad that I didn't bring him because the photos that I had given to my brother to give to her were not on the wall. I kept looking up at the wall feeling disheartened. She noticed and said they were up but the kept falling down so she had to have them taken down. My brother got her ready and we went to the market to do some shopping. We stopped for some food at KFC and my brother had to feed her. It felt uncomfortable but we just had to keep going and I didn't want to make her feel any more uncomfortable than she already felt. Then we had to take her to the toilet before we got back on the bus to

spread your wings, speak your truth, write it down & let it 116 go

go home. When we arrived outside the toilet, I attempted to wait outside but my mum told me to come in as they could do with the extra help. It was hard seeing what my brother had to do and to be up so close and personal with my mum when I had barely been this close to her before. Now I was having to adjust her sanitary because of that weird thing they do when you pull your knickers up.

My brother stayed but I came back home and was running late as me and my boyfriend were going out with another couple we knew. They were a bit annoyed by the time I got there though as the fair was closing so we didn't get to do much, but I had more important things going on internally. One thing the guy wanted to do though was go in the bungee ball. I wasn't keen as it horrified me the first time I went in there. My boyfriend was too high to go in and the guy's girl was pregnant as I was I late I jumped in to make up for it.

Months later my mum was taken into hospital after having a choking episode, her organs had started to deteriorate and at many points in the day she struggled to breath. It scary every time, when we talked on the phone that time it happened, she let out what sounded like a gasp and then there was nothing I was calling her down the phone suddenly she was back. I saw it happen whilst we were out too knowing there's nothing you can do and hope for the best that her breath comes back. This was how she died. The day she died my brother had gone to visit her in the hospital she told him she was going to die that day but he thought that she was just saying it through fear and so he did his best to reassure her in the hope she wouldn't give up. He said his goodbyes to her and made his way to the train station which was round the corner form the hospital. The hospital called my mums next of kin who was Levi.

He lived in London for as long as I could remember, we would go and stay there sometimes, and he and my mum got closer when she moved to London. On this occasion though he was not there when she needed him. The hospital called him to tell him to come in, but he chose not to go. When my brother found out what time the call was, he was devastatingly angry because he was only just getting on the train and had they of called him he would have gone back, and she would never have died alone.

During that day I had been feeling out of sorts and had no idea why. That same night I was unable to sleep then I heard my land line ringing. I laid still and said to myself if this important they will ring my mobile. The house phone rang again, and I knew then whoever was calling was calling to tell me about my mum. As I feared my mobile rang and it was my step aunty before she even had a chance to say anything I said, "my mums died hasn't she," my step aunty said yeah and asked how I knew, but I don't know how I knew but I did. After we hung up, I called my brother but there was no answer I stayed up all night and was ringing him for hours, call after call there was nothing. This was a strange set of circumstances as any other time I had needed my brother no matter the time he always answered. Any time there was an emergency with the kids he always just happened to be awake. I was calling him right into the next afternoon when he answered and had to break news to him that I thought he would be breaking to me. I felt his heartbreak in the silence of that moment before the tears fell from his eyes. As he cried, I cried, he was crying for his loss and the pain of that loss I was crying because my brother was crying. I didn't know how to feel.

Me, my brother, and our sister came together to go through the things that were left in the house and were told by Levi to go through all the paperwork and see if we could find any insurance documents. We never found any but I found something more important than that. A letter that my mum had written to Ashbert, it detailed how heartbroken she was about what he had done to me and not just to me but also to her. She had talked to him about what he had done to her and as a result of that conversation he had promised her that he wouldn't go near me in any way. Obviously, his word meant nothing.

Tears fell straight from my eyes on to the page now a lot more things made sense, and everything took a distinct perspective. I had been told before that maybe she had been through this, but I was too busy being angry. Taking the perspective that if that had of been the case then why did she not protect me from it. Instead, I had to suffer the same. I was little older now and had, had some work done of my own and whilst I still feel conflicted at times, I have a better understanding of her predicament.

We finished clearing the house and my brother's dad helped us bring some things back to Reading and we helped my sister to move into the flat she was given by the council. She had to be rehoused as they were in a 4 bed. We then had to have the difficult conversation about the sendoff we were going to have, not having a clue how to make these decisions and no adults to ask as they were all arguing. what about I don't even know no one had any right to take any claim over anything that belonged to my mum or her as a person. None of them had treated her with the respect she deserved, even her sister who it seemed like she was close to abandoned her in a distressing moment. Before my mums' body had started to completely fail her. She had gone to the toilet, but she had swelled up and had got stuck on the toilet. She called her sister who said she couldn't help her and left her sat there. My aunts' husband was the one who went who went round there and got her off the toilet after he had finished work. Who does that, just leaves their disabled sister on the toilet for hours on end knowing she can't move so she won't have eaten or drank and all the pain that she could have been in being stuck there for so long? Then having someone else come to your rescue you whilst you're not even decent, good job he was a good guy.

The decision was made by vote I voted to have my mum buried there was a saying my mum used to say that I couldn't remember whilst we were deciding and I didn't remember until it was way too late, and it was that you burn rubbish and bury gold. I was out voted, and the decision was made for her to be cremated. My nan wasn't impressed and when my mum went through the curtain, she screamed with all her might. But things must have been extra difficult for my nan in general at this time as not only had she lost her daughter but the year before Isiah had also died. He had a stroke and was taken into hospital just before hurricane Ivan. My nan struggled to get to see him during this phase and some of the roof was taken off their house and water came in, by the time she could get to the hospital again it was too late. She was devasted and was so unhappy because she hadn't got his tomb ready in time in the garden. This is a traditional thing to do in the Caribbean. We also thought we were going to lose my step aunty that year too as she was suffering from a Sickle Cell Crisis. She lived alone in Luton, but we spoke on the phone all of the time and this time in particular I could not get hold of her for love nor money. I started ringing other people I can't remember who exactly, but an ambulance was called, and she was taken to hospital. She had vomited on the carpet in her struggle and my aunt left it there for my aunt to clean up when she got back, which was about three days later.

When I went to the funeral, it was a highly unexpected emotional time for me personally. The day began with an incredibly early morning taking the kids to my friend's house before the school run, luckily, she had her mum to help her as she had three of her own children to look after. Me and Warren got on the train and made our way. We showed up at the house where we were greeted by a mixture of people some I didn't know. I was introduced to woman and straight after she was like well how could you turn up to your mum's funeral looking like that. I had on appropriate attire, but I wore my trainers with it for the journey I had proper shoes in my bag. which I told her, but I did think who, was she to tell me about what I was wearing. For all she knew that could have been all I had, imagine how bad I would have felt and there would have been nothing I could have done about it. I changed my shoes and went into the living room where my mum was laying inside her coffin, wearing her bridesmaids dress from when my aunt got married. Warren chose not to come in and waited in the hallway. I walked into the living and just had a moment where I just looked at her. It was like she was sleeping, and we were all there just waiting for her to wake up. Me and my siblings chose a song each and they were playing in the background. My sister had chosen Sean Pauls' Never gonna be the same. My brother chose Nas's feat Quan Just a moment and I chose Aaliyah's' Miss you. I cried and was comforted by my brother. I just wanted to rest my hand on her and say everything was alright. I touched her but couldn't say anything I was taken aback by how cold she was to the touch and that very same cold feeling stayed with me for weeks after. The time came to take my mum to the church and as they went to take her, I had a breakdown that I or no one else was expecting. I screamed and cried and collapsed in a heap of emotion my cousin, Ashbert's daughter was doing her best to hold me up. There was a point where I just went blank, I caught a glimpse of someone just watching me the more I noticed him the more I noticed others and I was blocking the door so it meant my mum couldn't be taken out until I moved. We went to the church in the funeral cars and when we got there my brother and our little cousin who I was close to when we were younger helped to carry the coffin in. I didn't know until I got there that I was doing a reading. We all stood together and took turns saying what my sister had organised. When I got to my piece, I felt hot and under pressure I looked up and saw all the people there just looking at us waiting for me to speak. I started the reading and then when I looked up again, I could see Ashbert just looking at me. I looked right back down at the page and kept going I was meant to stop for everyone else to repeat a biblical verse, but I didn't realise and powered through. My sister wasn't happy about this, but it was done so there was nothing I could do now.

The wake was back at my mum's house after it got started, I went round gathering the family together, well those who had bothered to stay, my aunt and Ashbert had already left. I'm guessing it was to avoid the meeting. We went up to one of the rooms and proceeded to read the letter that my mum had found from my mum to Ashbert, everyone was disgusted and disheartened. There was a moment that I became overwhelmed and began to cry, one of my step uncles rubbed my back in encouragement for me to keep going and I did. Levi burst into an outrage and blamed my little sister and said it's her fault our mum was dead. I don't know how he came to that conclusion because whatever she had been through from before was already weighing her down more than anybody could possibly know. My sister did make some mistakes and there were moments where she was awful to our mum, but it must have been a difficult time for her. She had always had the support of my mum and now that had been taken away from her through my mums' illness and no one was giving her any support.

After the funeral I made some big realisations about my mum and how she was and why she done some of things she done and had struggled. I soon came to realise that in all the years I had been trying to not be like my mum it was beginning to show that I was actually more like her than I cared to imagine. I was always there for people and bring people together by organising gatherings and trying to make the most out of life after being in a tough situation.

I already hated the Christmas period and New Year because of what had happened, and it was just made worse by the fact that my mum had died on the 5th of December. My mum had brought some Christmas gifts for my children but hadn't had the chance to give them to me, but my brother did. He had planned to stay home alone that year, but I didn't let him especially as he was blaming himself for our mum's death. He feels that if he had listened to her when she said she was dying things may have been different. I have done my best to reassure him that there was nothing he could have done and had the hospital of called him at the time he would not have hesitated to go back to the hospital instead of getting on the train. He came under the agreement that he could cook the dinner and so I agreed and that was our Christmas every year until my brother started spending Christmas with his dad and other siblings. I don't blame him for making this change either, things at mine weren't great, the last Christmas we spent together was full of drama as I found Warren was cheating again this time with the same woman again on the night, we were supposed to be wrapping the kids presents together. I caught him out a few times and it actually made sense as to why he was always accusing me even before I cheated that one time, which I hated myself for and have never done again since.

CHAPTER 11

When we moved into our upside-down house, there were a lot of people who hung around in the area. Some I already knew from growing up and some I got know from living there. After Warren lost his job as a glazier for committing benefit fraud, he got another one as loft insulator but then lost that too for smoking in the work van and failing his drugs test. Whilst he was unemployed, he was taken with the idea of working with the people who hung around outside our area and I have no idea why when he had plenty of trades experience, brick laying, glazing, and plastering. Had he of really looked he would have found a job no problem. Getting a CSCS card would have been no problem with all the experience he had. He went to the people outside and asked if he could work with them. Some of them had known me since I was a baby and had got to know my children and so didn't want us caught up in all the repercussions that came from it. So, they refused him using that very answer and explained that they only do what they do because they have to. But Warren was not satisfied with this and then began to set his mind to wanting to that job no matter what they said. I think they also had their own concerns as they knew that Warren was a problematic person from when we had one of our first arguments there and he slammed the front door into my face a bust open my top lip. I ran out of the house screaming and bleeding. My daughter and son were living room. The guys outside came to my rescue. They said they would have beat him up but when they did that for the last woman who lived there in that situation, she got mad with them and called the police on them and got back with her boyfriend. They checked with me where the kids were, and I told them they were inside, and they came with me to get them as my boyfriend was still in there. Well so I thought when he got in there he had gone and left the kids. I had gone in just in time as my first son was crawling and was at the top of the stairs. As I picked him up, I saw the hallway window open. Warren had gone down the stairs and climbed out. The guys stopped what were they were doing for while so I

spread your wings, speak your truth, write it down & let it 123
go

could call the police and get some help. Janine came to get me, and the kids and we stayed with her and Aimee. In the morning, my kids were too afraid to come near me because of how deformed my face looked. It was all swollen and the natural lines that formed from the center base of my nose into the top of my lip, which is called the philtrum had gone and there was just a big fleshy gap. The lines have permanently gone and now I just have a scar there instead.

Again, he went back and asked someone different they told him the same thing but told him that if he really couldn't find any work soon then they would let him come and work until he found something. He decided how long he was going to wait before going back to them. At this time, we were claiming joint benefits as I had been called into the benefit office by the fraud team who were quite reasonable and said that if I told her that I was living with someone since Christmas then she would let it go and we could make a joint claim form there then it would be fine. However, if I went ahead and made a statement which they found to be untrue then I would have to suffer the consequences. I felt like I was in a catch 22 situation, I instinctively wanted to speak out but then feared the repercussions of Warren's actions as he told me that no matter what they said not to admit anything as he wouldn't be happy if I did. When he was being violent, I never knew if it would be just an outrage where he was going to punch through the walls or if he was going to punch me, strangle me or threaten me with a knife. With that in my mind I followed his instructions. I wasn't believing it as they had evidence of bank statements and letters in his name with name my address. When he had the idea for me to claim alone, I told him it couldn't be done with him using me as his next of kin and my address instead of his mums. He went mad and accused me of trying to get his mum into trouble which I wasn't trying to do. He was unhappy with the decision that the Job Centre had made and decided that it was my fault too, the only thing that saved me that day was being able to tell him about the paperwork that they had as one piece was from his work. As he then felt he had his piece proof for who reported us. We were made to have a joint claim and pay back money to the amount totaling £14,000. This soon became solely my responsibility as when he went to prison, he denied having anything to do with it. Even though he had the cheek to still my using my address in the hope of being released back to it.

Also now being distracted by getting the job with the guys outside which was just meant to be until he found something else which he had no intention of doing, we just got on with things. It was okay at first, he was helping to provide, and we would go out and do things. Any time the police came in the area he would either run inside or hide outside depending on where they were or when they came. I hated this but there was not much I could do about it and on the plus side this meant he always had money for weed so I didn't have to borrow from my family to stop him from having a melt down when we didn't have any. I smoked too but I wasn't like him with it. I guess giving up throughout my pregnancies made it easier for me to go without when we didn't have any. I got back into smoking again after my mum died to help me sleep at night as I every time I closed my eyes all I could see was my mums' face and it scared me. The downside was that it always meant he had money for alcohol, which means he spent more time being drunk. He seemed as though he felt more of a man when he had a drink even though he didn't act like one, it's like it enabled him to more of the things he wanted do, but on many, many occasions this always went too far but he never seemed to regret anything enough to make him even try to stop and the rest of the time he was so drunk he couldn't remember things or at least so he says anyway. We had been together for 10 years by this point so now it just looked as the though the drink gave him the courage to be who he was every day and that happened not to be a very a nice person and he knew this and knew a lot of his ways were wrong, but everyone always put his behaviour down to being drunk so it was like he was always excused. But the pattern I see is he needed Dutch courage everyday so he could behave as he pleased. This became more apparent to me when I had our fourth child. The pregnancy in itself was difficult and so was the labour. This time I had symphysis pubis dysfunction again and sciatica and struggled to move altogether without any pain and it meant I couldn't have a bath unless my boyfriend was home to help me. We paid Aimee's' friend to do the nursery drop off and pick up. Warren spent most of his time down at a radio station that his friend had, the most time spent together was when he had the snip as it meant he had to be home for two weeks to recover. He had it in good time, so he was ready for when I went into labour. He was adamant he did not want any more kids but as I learnt later this made it easier for him to sleep around as no one would be able to say they were pregnant by him. Although that didn't stop one girl, but I will touch more on that later.

This labour was another planned home birth but was taking a lot longer than they expected it with it being my fourth child. I had a temperature and was starting to feel unwell, so the midwife called an ambulance, and I was taken into hospital. One of the neighbour's was shouting something out of the window but I was too focused on being in labour and in too much pain to hear her. But Aimee did though but she kept it to herself and didn't say anything because it wasn't the right time. I got to the hospital where the doctors and midwives were arguing about what I should or shouldn't be doing. Some wanted me to push, and some didn't want me to because I was only 9cms dilated so still had a centimeter to go. The pain was different in this labour to the point it brought tears to my eyes. Whilst labour pain is beyond painful for me it didn't usually bring tears. This time I had an infection, the year after this whilst under the care of gynecologist for menorrhagia and painful periods I found out I had PID so this could have been what was causing the problem. the baby had meconium filled waters but a lot more filled than the others were. I was just doing what my body was telling me, which was to push, I committed to doing it because I knew my body could manage as they estimated that this baby would be born the same size as they last. But they were so wrong. I gave birth to a baby that weighed a healthy 10lb 4oz at half past two on a Friday afternoon. Aimee and Janine were at this birth with my boyfriend when we got to the hospital Aimee waited outside and Janine came into the room. They went to get the older two from school and my brother came and took the little one out after collecting him from nursery. Me and Warren had that time to spend with the baby and he used that time to complain that I had gone into labour when I did because he had plans to go and me having the baby meant he couldn't go now. Anybody would have thought I had gone into labour on purpose, to stop him from going out.

I told him if that was how he felt then he should just get up and go.

He said, "well I can't now I because imagine how bad that will look."

And there it was he wanted to do something but couldn't because of how it looked, and he didn't want to look bad, had he of at a drink though he would have gone anyway. I think he did get his way in the end because I was kept in overnight due to how meconium filled the waters were as they had to be careful that the meconium does not go in his lungs as it can harden up. I was kept in again the next day as well as they found he had a slight heart murmur which disappeared within 24hours.

He made a choice like this again at a later date. I was washing up and had the youngest two at home the baby was sat on the floor, but I couldn't hear him when I turned round, I saw he was going blue. I picked up and called the doctors and got my third child's shoes on and we went to the doctors. The doctor decided we should go to the hospital as he suspected he had meningitis. I called my boyfriend on the way and told him I needed him to leave work because I was taking our son to hospital with suspected meningitis, he refused. So, I called my brother and always I was able to rely on him in times like this, he left his work as soon as he could and came and took my third child. Sadly my third son was already upset by the time he was able to get there because at this point the baby had been injected through his stomach to get to his bladder as he wasn't urinating, he had a canula in his arms blood was taken, he was screaming and crying and fighting the doctors to the point where in the end we couldn't see him due to the amount of doctors that were huddled around him trying to hold him down and get done what they needed to find out what was wrong. His temperature was up to 41 degrees and rising and his heart rate was so fast that if he had been adult he would have been classed as having a heart attack. He ended up staying in hospital for a week. The only thing they were able to diagnose was bronchiolitis, I was told there was nothing more they could do as they were not able to find anything else wrong and they didn't what else to do or say as medically I should be going home without a baby as he should be dead. They gave me a piece of paper with the ward phone number on it and said if anything else happens during the next 24hours then I could call the number and bring him in. Thankfully, I never had to. whilst I was dealing with the fact that our child had nearly died my boyfriend was going out to the radio, he did his bit with the kids in between Janine and Aimee helping out. But when I got home, he went out, to go out of his way to go to Tilehurst to pick up a girl he had been talking to whilst at the radio and take her to his radio set with him in Hurst. Instead of coming he went to Don's house where he got a bollocking from Don's dad as there was no getting out of what he had done he had a love bite on his neck as big as a hand. As that's what Don's dad did, gave us all advice and did his best to keep us in line along with his own kids. He came home and I felt myself crumbling from the inside out and had my first ever hyperventilation panic attack. He tried to calm me down, but I didn't want him near me and plus he had to go out anyway as he had to take his brother home from his guitar lesson. Which he used to pick him up and drop him off for as he lived in Slough and the lessons were in Reading.

We started to get things back on track and going out with our friends again. I'm surprised anyone went out with us at this point as there was always some sort of drama whenever we came even at his cousins wedding party he couldn't behave, I felt bad but had to defend myself as best as I could, it didn't help that he got others involved this time telling him that I had lost our eldest son when I hadn't our friend, who had been my aunts friend had taken him home with her as he sometimes stayed with her and her son that she now had. It was Don who approached so that was fine as I never felt threatened by him, but the point was, Warren was in his usual drunken state and yet still managed to have other people questioning what I was doing, like I was the one too drunk to know what was going on.

As I was saying we started going out with our friends again we were all having a goodnight and got kebabs on the way home. I decided to start eating mine in the car as we were dropping everyone off then Warren started going mad calling me a fucking bitch and asking me what the fuck, I thought I was doing. I was baffled and asked him what he meant.

"Look at ya, you're eating my fucking kebab. I wasn't at all his one was still in the bag which I told him and the others in the car intervened. That kept me safe until I got home, where it was just me and him. Thinking though that I would still be okay as I had his kebab in the bag and still had some of mine left. Unfortunately, it then became about the kebab in the bag not being his and how it was meant to be mine and I had eaten his. But I hadn't we exactly the same kebabs. He wasn't having any of it and wouldn't stop shouting at me and then he started hitting me. I tried ducking and diving he had me in a corner and without thinking I just charged into him in an attempt to get him to move so I could get out. That got us into the centre of the living room I went to run out of the door, and he grabbed me and pulled me back and was hitting me again in the scuffle I managed to get him to the door and open it all whilst he was hitting me. It was so manic I couldn't even tell you how or what order anything happened in, but I managed to get him onto the ridge of the doorstep. We were stuck fighting there and he lost his footing, or I managed to get him out not sure which one and with that he smashed his can of stella into my left eye so hard it crushed with the impact. In one of his arms retractions, I managed to slam the door shut and lock it so he couldn't get back in. I called one of the couples we had just been with, and the girlfriend told me to come to them and she called the police, or I did but either way they came out to their house to speak to me. That was the first time that anyone in our friendship circle had seen the outcome of anything he had done to me. They didn't have a clue what to say. The kids weren't home that night they were with Janine. After I gave my statement to the police, Selina had now been rehoused and it wasn't far from where the couple lived and as the couple had their own kids to get up for and it wasn't fair for their children to see me like that if we could help it. In the morning I went to collect the kids. The day I collected the kids I went home and my little sister from my dad's side had come to see me as she often did, since they were allowed contact me after their mum split with our dad. She stayed with me that night, which so good she did as I woke up in a panic as I couldn't see in my left eye everything was all dark. I don't know how long this went on for but once I could see again, I calmed down. I had to go to the hospital for some tests. The liquid that they put in to clean the eye really stung, it turns out he had grazed the skin around my eyeball. My eyeball had also sunk in further than it should be and the prescription on my glasses for my left eye had to change. Now whenever I go for an eye test it comes up as the damage to my eye can still be seen by them. We split up for a while after this and he was sleeping in the car outside after staying with a friend for a few days.

As I write this, I'm sat wondering what the hell was I doing and how and why was I putting up with all this. Well not really why but how. I know why and that's because I was brought up to be worthless so felt worthless and acted worthless and had no boundaries because any discipline, I had was not really discipline it was just to keep me in line with what they wanted me to do. He was treating me how I had always been treated but those where love should have been a more natural and better bond. From the little I know of my family history it seems this has been the line that has been followed for quite some time. With my nan being a product of rape, we can only imagine what followed down from the lines before.

Me in the upside-down house

We got an offer in for a move from the upside-down house, we talked and agreed this would be a fresh start but for him it just ended up being a new place to start more bullshit. He spent more time down in the old area even when he didn't need to be there. He was drinking even more than he used not that even seemed like it was possible he already used to get through seven to eight cans at a time downing them like they're water on a daily, so I dread to think how much more he was getting through. More of his outburst started to take place whilst he was down in our old area and so he caused problems down there alongside smashing up the local petrol station.

He started talking to more girls whilst he was down there one of which used to where blue eyeshadow, my friend Selina had seen it happening. Selina managed to find out who she was and where she lived as she had seen her at another friend's house and warned her off. I indirectly confronted Warren with Selina, we put on the same blue eyeshadow and did our hair exactly the same as the girl wore it. When he came home, he was shocked and didn't know what to say. He became even more unsettled when I said I needed him to look after the kids so I could go on a course that was on South Street, which was the same road the girl lived on. He was a bit lost for words and was just like yeah that should be fine. One morning I had gone to do the school run and as I left, I saw he had bothered to come home but never made it into the house. I opened the car door, and his phone rang so I answered it and it was a girl. She got shook and hung up the phone. Warren was in no fit state to drive us to school, so we had to catch the bus. This became a regular thing until he stopped coming all together because he got talking to another woman who was also working in the area. Selina said she could see it coming and we just let him get on with it whilst watching everything he done, like him only coming home to have a shower, always staying out but saying he was at one of the guy's houses and letting her do his washing, which he was curious to know how I figured it out. Which isn't hard when you think about it. I didn't have any proof of anything, but I knew I would catch him out in the end I just had to be patient. Warren, Selina, and another person we knew at that time were planning a party for my birthday. They went somewhere to look at a place for the party and Warren had left his phone behind and it went off and there it was my proof, I took photos of the messages and then put the phone back exactly as he left it. I didn't utter a word of it when he got back, I just carried on as if everything was fine.

We had the party, and she was obviously upset that he hadn't come home and was messaging him. We both had to sleep in the car that night as he had lost the keys. He was still asleep when the messages came through, so I text the girl back and told her everything was over as he decided to come home now. I sent it as though it came from him and then deleted it. When he woke up, he broke the back window of the house so we could get back in. We called his friend who was a glazier, and he fixed the window for us. He went to see the girl anyway he came up with the excuse that he had left a record there and needed to go and get it before she done something to it. I knew it was a lie and that he was gonna go there at some point anyway and just let him go anyway. Told him to make sure he was back in time for when the guy comes to clean up the garden, reason being he was known for being interested in children he even told Warren that to his face telling him if a little 8-year-old girl is out in a belly top then you know she's up for it. Warren clearly didn't find this disturbing enough to not want him in the garden of the house where his children lived, to clean up the dog shit of the dog he went behind my back to get after I said no when he begged me to get it because I knew he wouldn't look after it the way he should and there was no way I was struggling with a puppy and a baby. Warren's stance was that if he did or tried anything then he would just beat him up or kill him. Great but how does that help or change anything our child would have been through had anything of happened. I had already told Aimee's boyfriend that I couldn't manage with their puppy anymore even though he came round every day to look after it.

The person selling the puppies was Dons dad and even he had told Warren he wasn't going to sell him one because he doesn't even look after his own kids. Sadly, Don's dad died, we were all devasted and anyone in our social group at this time miss him dearly. Warren used this opportunity to get what he wanted, and he brought the puppy and took it home after the wake. His excuse was he was doing our mate a favour as he needed the money now. I told him that was fair enough but if he valued him that much as a friend, he could have given him the

spread your wings, speak your truth, write it down & let it go 132

money anyway and let him keep the dog so he could sell it to someone else and then he'd be able to have more money, which surely would have been better for him. As I suspected he didn't take care of the dog properly or train it and only walked it until the novelty wore off. The dog chewed everything, shoes the kids' toys, the seatbelts in the car because of days when he didn't want to out without the dog even though it meant the dog had to stay in the car. He left it outside and someone called the RSPCA. The dog got hit and kicked it got to the point where even the dog would hide when he came in drunk. Me and the kids loved the dog, but the reality of the situation was we didn't have time for one. My priority was the children which, we now had four of and where he was never home, I was basically doing everything alone. It was much the same as being a single parent with a regular sex partner on the side that was abusive and violent.

The worst occasion was having to have a home visit from the teachers of, the school that the kids were going to. It should have been a good occasion as they were coming to see us in a new house, but the dog had done his business in the middle of the floor in the boys' bedroom. I called my boyfriend to come and clear it up, but he refused. Luckily, it didn't get reported I think they could see I was a decent person in a troubled situation. Just like when social services were called after yet another domestic resulting in the police being called out and them informing social services. The social worker that came out looked at me and said he was surprised to see a woman like me in a situation like this as it didn't seem like the sort of thing I would put up with. I can see now he could see my strength that I was blind to at the time, that's how it was though people in authority could see my strength and so therefore did not see or understand my weakness. Others saw my vulnerabilities and were either blind, chose to see or willing tried to destroy my strengths. None of it made sense really, as Warren was bringing everything to our household that I had wanted to avoid. I had set out to build a happy home with a loving man as the father of my children. This isn't what we were getting but out of fear and downtroddeness and the good moments in between. I was struggling to get out. I always saw the good moments as a turning point and no matter what he always told me

spread your wings, speak your truth, write it down & let it 133
go

he loved me. We would have nice family days out that even ended on a nice note. But when you start to see that the bad is outweighing the good and the bad in one incident is enough to over a power a good week then you're on your way to being done for. No amount of flowers, wine, chocolate, perfumes, money or loving and I love yous will ever be able to make up for or compare to the outcome of a busted or bruised face or body and all that comes with it like, your children not being able to look at you if have them, not being able to look at yourself in the mirror, others looking at you with that look in their eyes and the embarrassment and humiliation that comes with that, especially when they see how often it happens. In the end you become so broken you don't even look up at people when you look like that. The questions asked by the children's school and the fact that it is written down in their files so now you know they are always watching you and questioning your parenting because of what you're letting go on in your household. At these times they don't care how well you have taught your child to read or how much you help with their homework or how on time they are for school or how much care you give them from your heart and how good you are with your child's appearance. Because do

you know what in grand scheme of things none of that matters when they are sat in school all day being withdrawn and unable to focus on the lesson because they're too busy worrying if mummy is okay at home and what she will look like when she picks you up from school. Or because they haven't been able to sleep the night before because of the constant arguing shouting, screaming and beatings knowing they desperately want to save their mum but daddy is much bigger than them so they know they can't. they don't forget this though either. When I managed to find the tools and my strength to get away and we became comfortable without him one the first things they said was "we should have saved you mummy". Words a child should never have to say to a parent let alone have to feel they should do. It also explained the deep liking of superheroes.

He was spending more and more time with her, so I decided to go and see her one day not to fight as he was the one who was destroying the home not her, but just see who she was and what she was about, and I took the kids with me so she could see what she was interfering with. At first, she accused them of not all being his but the longer we stayed the more apparent it became to her that they all were. We talked and then me and the kids left. I think she was confused but my visit played on her mind. We stopped sleeping together but still spoke and he still came round and sometimes we would still argue like when he got so drunk, he forgot to bring his kids dinner. He told me he never made that mistake and that I was nothing but fat bitch who only cared about food and that was why we were so broke because all I did was spend the money on take away. Which was laughable really as he was the one who had the drink and drug habit. After that I never asked him for a penny and so if I didn't have me and the kids went without and if they needed anything I waited 'til I had the money for it to get. He done a disappearing act and my middle sister Zuwena, who shared the same dad as me and my older sister but a different mum to us both was driving at the time, and I asked her if she could drive to the area where the girl lived and see if she could see my car. The one that had been brought for by my step aunty and my mums compensation money so he could get us about as a family not for him to act the fool with. Anytime I asked anyone to do that it was there even when he said he was going to stop seeing her and come home, which he did for a while but soon went back there. So now I had more proof. When he did that Selina came to sit with me and watched the kids, we stayed awake for the night and in the morning, I walked down to the area and stood and waited. It was a good few hours before he came out. I didn't know where he was going to come out from, so I stood where my car was in sight and then my moment came, and he appeared. He realised he had forgot something and went back for it, so I ran to the passenger side of the car and when I heard the unclicking of the lock, I opened the door and jumped in the car at the exact same time as he did. Can you believe this guy had the cheek to say to me what did I think I was doing down there as I should be at home looking after the kids like I wasn't the one always doing that anyway? He only spent time with them when he felt like it which was now even rarer than usual and even then, that would end in us fighting if I had to pull him up on the way he was speaking to them. Like when he called one of our sons a pussy after he winded him with the football to the point he was going blue in the face, another time when our son fell on the plug of the extension lead warren started having a go at him even though it was Warren that had left it there in the first place. Going mad at all of them if they weren't playing the console games the way he wanted them to and even more so when if they lost the game. In the end it put them off the game, they didn't even pay it after he left.

He continued to drive us home where we had yet another argument this time, he didn't hit me, but I had hit him in the face in car after I had caught him out and made that comment to me.

There were more nights like this where he was to and fro from the house the only time it really bothered me again was on my mums on anniversary, he was meant to bring me back something to smoke so I could sleep but instead he took the money I gave him and spent it on the weed but took it to her house and smoked it with her instead. Then had the audacity to turn up at mine in the morning with the girls last spliff, which in fact was probably mine as it was probably from what he gave her from the money I gave him. That made her mad and she decided to text me to say that she thinks that he has been playing us both. I knew he had been the whole time, but I said to her we should confront him together I told her to pick me and what time. She never asked where from but turned up at my house right on time, confirmation that she knew where I lived and had been dropping off to see the kids now that we didn't have a car as he decided to scrap it. Funny thing was though I wasn't allowed to know where she lived when I had asked him. She drove us in her lovely little sports car down to the area where he worked, and we approached him at the same time. He had a message to say that we were both coming, he went to run but it was too late.

"You thought we wouldn't find out, didn't you?" She shouted

I didn't have time for words I switched into some kind of mad animal and started attacking him and he stood there and took it. I made him give me half the weed he had. When I looked back at her she was in

spread your wings, speak your truth, write it down & let it 136
go

shock and was worried I was going to turn on her instead I replaced the weed he had taken from her plus a little bit more. As whilst she was willing sleeping with a man who was in a relationship with the mother of his children, she wasn't to know that the weed she was sat smoking with him was meant to be for me on night that I was struggling with emotions about my mum. I got a lift home from someone else, and Selina had stayed with the kids.

He came home again after that, but things were dying out between us. He organised another party for me for my 30th birthday and got people to chip in for a stretch hummer and hired the VIP lounge in the club. It was a great night we had champers in the hummer, and I had drinks on tap all night. I'm not usually sick when I drink but this night I was and, but I carried on right back after. By the end of the night, I had the mic, and the club was poppin' even now when I think about it, I have to say it was definitely an enjoyable time. He managed to cause trouble as usual but this time it didn't involve me, so I just let him get on with it.

When it was time to go home, we realised that he had been arrested and the hummer had gone because of whatever stunt it was he pulled.

The next day he called me from the police station saying he had lost his phone and that he was now on his way home but was going to be a while as he had to walk. He said he was sorry about what had happened but at this point I wasn't even phased, and his phone wasn't lost he had left it in my bag, so I had it and right on cue just like the last time, which was only a year before, she texts him. I didn't say anything I just stayed quite for a few days and started to keep my distance.

I came down one night to see he had left a bud on the table, I picked it up and placed my engagement ring on it placed it back down on the table and went back up to bed. He asked what it's about when he got in and I told him to figure it out. We kept our distance whilst only making small talk he stayed downstairs and I stayed up, he only came upstairs when there was a night that felt off like something was happening. He had the same feeling. He came upstairs and said he was unsure as to whether he should go down to the old area. I said no I didn't think he should. He didn't go but the actions he took the following day he may as well of just went down there and got it over with. As that night the whole area got raided and shutdown and multiple arrests were made. Others got picked up from their house the next day, but he had to be stupid and go down there and go drunk as well. He had just found out from the lady who lived in our old house what had happened, as he was leaving, he took it upon himself to put his finger up at a police car that went past. They saw him and went back for him; he ran into the woman's house, and they went in after and said to him they had been looking for him. Whilst they were arresting him, he is shouting at the woman to record the arrest. Not that it would have made a difference because he was going down anyway. Whilst I felt bad for the women for what he had done I was glad that my kids didn't have to see any of it.

My youngest had started school and as I had said many times before as soon as they were old enough, I would go to work so that's what I did. I started volunteering in the school, which meant I wasn't home whilst he had to be because there was nowhere for him to go whilst he was awaiting trial. Well, I guess he could have caught up with his old friends that he hadn't seen in a while due to his changed lifestyle. In fact, he did catch up with them in the end as I got to a place where I was strong enough to end the relationship and he had stopped hitting me now. It's amazing what pressing charges can do to someone. He ended up destroying those friendships due to his drunken behaviour in the end they didn't want him around because of how he was when he was drunk, not only was his attitude bad he also stole from them.

The night of the proposal and engagement party, that smile had been wiped off my face by the end of the night. It ended in Janine, Aimee and her boyfriend having to stay with me and the kids so that Warren couldn't have his drunken meltdown in the house and attack me.

I wasn't really home before this anyway, but he wasn't around to notice. At first it was just mainly Mondays that I was out as I would take the children to a playgroup down at the back of the school church. It was run by a lady vicar and soon she was needed to fulfil other duties as the main church vicar had sadly passed away. The lady vicar then turned to me and asked me how I felt about leading the playgroup. I felt honoured to be asked but also shocked that she would want someone like me running the place and organising trips and being in charge of money. Not that I couldn't be trusted but more the fact I was being looked at as a trusted person rather than someone who was gonna ruin things. I enjoyed running the group and organising trips for us to go on. I was always at the school café. The school had a new vicar and he had come up with the idea of using the area at the back of the church as a café is the mums didn't have to stand outside in the rain whilst they had a chat in the morning. It was great the place had a kitchen and a big room where the vicar had set out tables and chairs. There were toys for the children who were not yet in school to play with, he also provided biscuits and sometimes someone would bring cake. He was a nice guy and was easy to talk to. We had many chats about many different topics as he did with many. We had two lady vicars before him, and they all joined forces and worked together. I felt close to them all and the time came for to get my files from social services it was them I went to for support. I sat them down and gave them my life story and explained what I wanted to do next. There wasn't a dry eye in the room, it felt like a face palm emoji moment. This is not the reaction I was expecting it's not comforting being able to silence a room like that. They told me I was brave and said they would support me through. Well at least two of them did anyway. One of the lady vicars left as she was not happy with her position. The one who stayed had helped me from the offset, I don't know what it was about me that she did, but I am forever grateful to her. It was thanks to her that myself and my children got more days out and never suffered when it came to finances. She even babysat a few times and paid for me and Warren to have therapy sessions that he didn't bother to turn up to. Me being the most verbal made it easier for her to pick up that I had a lot of unresolved issues especially when he was late for one of our appointments choosing to travel to Twyford at the time of the appointment to see a friend when he should have come to the appointment first and then went to see his friend after. He came to the appointment with 10 mins to spare. The therapist gave me a chance to say my piece and he didn't have much to say. But of course, I was angry someone had taken time out of their life to come and sit in ours and paid for us to have sessions to help our relationship. the least he could do was turn up.

Me leading a playgroup trip

Him being at home all the time was making him insecure and the more I was needed at the school the longer I started to stay. He refused to believe that I would be there for so long without being paid but I did and I'm glad as it started to pay off as they soon employed me. The arguments started again as the small talk turned it into snide remarks, he started going to through my Facebook and then had a go at one of my friends because I liked his picture. The photo was of him at a photo shoot, it was a good picture, and I didn't even like the guy like that he was just an old school friend. Anyway, the guy either removed himself or Warren removed him, I just let him carry on and tried not to let anything he said get to me. I did well apart from three occasions, I was holding back tears when he told me that he hopes I get cancer and die. The other time we were sat downstairs he was at the desk, and I was sat on the sofa, he wanted to know if everything was okay because I wasn't having sex with him, I told him with all that had gone on I just wasn't interested in it. He said that was very unlike me and that if I didn't have sex with him soon, he would just go and have sex with someone else. I told him to go ahead because that what he usually does anyway even if I am having sex with him, so I don't know what was stopping him. He said he didn't want to. After a gap of silence, he then said, "I'm sorry for what I've done to you, but I think I only did it because I could because I knew no one was gonna come and get me and beat me up because you had no one to do that for you." My brother would have if he had tried it at a time that he was there, he knew I could handle myself but always had my back when it came down to it. I couldn't believe my ears after a moment of shock I got up and left the room. He then became shocked and said "what! What's your problem? I was just being honest I thought that would work you always want me to be honest." Which was true but it didn't mean I had to like it. The issue got worse when my daughter came to me in fear because he kept looking at her funny as he had told her something and he had started to think she had told me. But up until this point she hadn't but his words were "your mum is nothing but a victim, she always has been and always will be."

We became even more distant after that, we had another argument where he got a knife out, I ran screaming outside, the police came but I don't remember if it was myself or a neighbour who called them. He tried saying he got the knife out for himself, but I wasn't going to take any more risks and it was a shock to the system as he didn't really try to hit me again after what he done to my eye because the police pressed charges on him, he had a fine to pay and community service to do. He tried throwing in my face once, but I told him should never have hit me in the first place then he wouldn't be in this predicament. I kept him out the house after that being sure to call the police every time, he came round that was the only way to stop him and I had to what I could because then he started damaging neighbour's property taking slabs from their walls to try and break the window so he could get in. The school that the children went to, where I also worked, started letting us come in early and late and leaving early so we could avoid him at all possible costs. He soon went to court about the raid that took place I our old area and was sentenced. The day before I let the children go with my friend who was my neighbour in the flats take them to see him, she said it was emotional but so was seeing the damage he had caused by his behaviour and by me not having the tools required to leave sooner than I did.

As soon as he had gone inside, we had support put in place and worked with a family support worker and counsellors which helped to bring us together as a family without him. Then it was all printed in the local paper and our daughter started to get comments made towards at her

spread your wings, speak your truth, write it down & let it 142
go

school about it as they printed the pictures of the people in the paper and the road names of where they lived. The problem with our situation was that he didn't live there anymore. I called the courts to discuss this with them and they said there was nothing they could do even though it was having an impact on the children at school. I spoke to the ladies' service that was helping us and they done some investigating to find that he had gone to prison using my address. Had we not of found that out he would have been released back to my house and I would have been stuck again as they were released with curfews and area restrictions. Thankfully the lady was able to get this issue resolved.

Life was peaceful for the 8 months he was away, and I enjoyed it being just me and the kids and they missed having the dog. But we did a lot more socialising and spending time at friends' houses without having to worry about what we were going to have to come home too. We stayed at their houses, and they stayed at ours and we had a laugh.

I met someone new but that didn't last, it turned out he had a girlfriend with a baby on the way I sent a letter to his house after not hearing from him for a little while. My friend who was my neighbour in the flats told me where he lived after she figured out who he was. He definitely received the letter because he was making calls to call things off with people and he rang me twice by accident, he called at first to say he couldn't see me no more. Then he called again thinking he was calling someone different and said, "yeah some stupid bitch sent a letter to my house init so I can't see you no more." "Oh, so there was more than one of us then what a good job I did it, I'm the stupid bitch who sent the letter." The line went quiet and then dead. I had an unexpected reading about this too, I was having a catch up on messenger with a woman who had been a friend of my mum. Mid conversation she started telling me about someone in my relationship had been cheating for a year. Which was obviously Warren, she then went on to say that the person I was dealing with now could not be trusted as he wasn't being honest with his intentions. She also let me know that a Gemini friend of mine was not being the friend she had appeared to be. She also let me know that my step uncle was watching over me.

spreað your wings, speak your truth, write it ðown & let it 143 go

Me and my friends started going out which I enjoyed and ended up going more than anyone else and no one would want to come so then I started going out alone. There was always someone there I knew so I wasn't too bothered, and I could always handle myself. I only needed to defend myself twice that I can recollect. One man was trying to feel me up at the bar telling me about how he'd always fancied a bit of black. Well, he wasn't getting any of me I fought him off and threw a drink in his face. I knew it was time to stop going out when I was fighting with men for stealing my drinks. I tried dating apps to find they were not for me either guys were abusive if you didn't let them come to you when they wanted or they were basically looking for somewhere to live or a place to stay when they came into town. The funniest experience I had was arranging to go out for dinner and then getting to the date for the man to tell me that he had already eaten as he likes to eat by a certain time and now was too late for him. But he was happy to pay for me to eat whilst he watched. Like what kind of stupidness is that. I was like I'm cool thanks, with conversation being drier than the wine I left. He wasn't impressed that I was leaving and refused to let him give me a lift because I was supposed to trust him because he was a Christian. I kept walking and hopped on the bus got myself a kebab and went to my friend's house where me kids and my old neighbour was and chilled with them. Baffled as to why I had gone for dinner and come back with a kebab I filled them in on what had gone on.

I made friends with a guy, but he was just looking for somewhere different to hide out as he was sleeping with his baby mum's best friend. The only time I went out after that was for work dos, I was fully employed now as they were so impressed with my skills that were shown during my volunteering and a temporary placement that they gave me with a young boy who had autism. They asked me to work with him until they found someone else who could do the role from a professional background. I was given support and it turned out that not only did they not find anyone to take the role on I was doing a good job and kept him going until he left the school. That then became my role when required other times I was a Teaching assistant working either one to one or with small groups of children to help boost their understanding, I was also good at covering classes on the very odd occasion. This job had given me a new lease of life, I was needed and able to help others and praised and was good at something all positives. The role became a bit conflicting when the school got involved in my personal life as my children attended the same school and the breakdown in relationship with their dad meant that the children were affected, and this had an impact on their schooling. Also, by now I had learnt about all of the surrounding services that schools use for support when they are helping children. So, when the relationship broke down, I went to the school and requested a support worker and other services so they could help me, and my children stay safe. This involved many, many meetings where sometimes they were supportive and other times I felt just as bullied as I did in my relationship when I was being assaulted and emotionally abused. In the end I had a severe panic attack, which took a lot of energy and was hard to recover from. Which was not surprising because when you are in a team around the child meeting the last thing you expect is to be attacked when you are the main one supporting the children and asking for the extra help to be protected from the abusive person. Especially when at this point, he had been emotionally abusive to the children and all you are hearing is that you are bitter and start telling you that you need to separate yours and his relationship from the relationship of his and the children's. At first, I did not understand how they could not see what was there right in front of their eyes. He was playing the long game of doing what was right so he could get what he wanted. Him being unhappy about being made to go elsewhere when he came out of prison, I believe was his drive. When he got out, he was seen in town by my daughters then best friend and her mum and had asked them not to say they had seen him. But obviously with them being our friends they did let us know; it was the same day as my mum's birthday, so this just made the day worse. He was getting support from a company who help those who are addicts, homeless and released from prison. He played by all their rules and even done a sponsored homeless sleep to help raise money for the charity. The lady from the company who was supporting him rang the school and asked if he could come and see the children. My boss at the time explained to her that it didn't work like this especially with all that

spread your wings, speak your truth, write it down & let it 145 go

had gone on. She invited the lady to the school for a meeting with me and my boss and the emotional support worker from our school. Where they basically talked me into letting the father of my kids see the kids as it was in all our best interests especially because if he took me to court it would go in his favour. I reluctantly gave in under the condition that the visits would take place at school and be supervised by both parties the visits started off well but there were a few times where he had to be spoken to about some minor inappropriate behaviour's that he had around the children during his visiting times. Part of me grateful for the school doing this but the other part of me was not because I knew what it was going to lead into and in fact, he went right into that and beyond. Which didn't really surprise me because I knew he had everybody fooled all the women in the room were wearing their old victim statuses from their previous situations and just reacted based on their own fear and stresses that had been brought up for them, which I get but as professionals they should have checked their facts. Even more so knowing that the house was a red spot on the police radar and us having a panic alarm fitted for anytime he was outside the house. All they could see was that everything was about me instead of seeing who he was as a person. No one wonder narcissists believe they have so much power, it's because they get away with everything, they do for so long so when the game that only they are playing doesn't go their way they lose their shit so badly or learn to play a longer game.

The visits continued in school until the summer holidays where we had to start having them outside of school because obviously school was closed. I knew things were going to get worse and he had already been saying to the kids that when he finds out who I'm seeing he is gonna kill him and that they're gonna get up for school one day and see his head one a fence post or hanging from the door frame. What a lovely thing to say to your children just because you can't keep your jealousy to yourself and accept that you are the reason the relationship has ended. This went on a lot him saying things to the kids or getting them to tell him things about what I was doing. Every time they went with him, I was spending the time that they were with me having to undo all of the work that he had done and get them back into routine. Some of the

spreað your wings, speak your truth, write it ðown & let it go 146 counselling the kids had done had started to become undone although some of it didn't help anyway as they were saying to the kids that dad can't always be to blame and asking are there things that mum could do differently to stop the arguments. Not quite sure what the aim was here but when your mum is getting smacked up for eating a kebab or being called names for no reason other than the dad being an insecure alcoholic or being spoken to aggressively because he's ran out of weed and had an extra few. I'd like to know what they think the mum should do to stop this because other than leaving when you finally find the strength to, being submissive seems to be the only solution here. Which is just as damaging for the children to see so still don't even see how that helps.

As I suspected he became more verbally abusive towards me and the children, the visits slowed down and stopped being stuck too, this made the kids frustrated as they would make plans but then on the day, he turned up he would expect them to go with him. This carried on until the absolute worst happened, he came to pick them up and took them to a dessert parlour in the area where he lived. They chose what was familiar from the menu as they had been to this dessert parlour with me in their hometown. So, they ordered what they knew they liked obviously thinking it would be the same. What they ordered wasn't quite what they were used to it being so when he asked what their problem was with the food my daughter explained. He was not happy, but neither were they as not only had he turned up a weekend late with no explanation, which they believe was to do with the girl who was shouting out of her window whilst I was in labour as it transpires, she had slept with him, and they were now seeing each other. They also weren't happy that they had to change their plans so last minute and not happy with their dessert waffles that came out watery. He went out in a huff to have a fag when he came back in, they left and went back to his house where he drank and got drunk with his dad. He then punched my middle son in his face so hard it was bruised. The children said it started off as play fighting but they could see he was getting rough and out of hand but there was nothing they could do and they didn't know what to do in terms of, making contact for help because he was always looking at their phones when they were on them. They said once he realized what he did he told our middle son to punch him back. Once it had all calmed down, he decided it was a clever idea to drink drive and take them bowling. The kids said they were scared because they knew he was drunk and hadn't even realized that he drank like that anymore as he had changed his brand of beer and told them he was drinking energy drinks. I had a feeling he was still drinking but what could I do when no one was listening to me about how he was. Even the police were saying they weren't surprised by his behaviour at the times he hadn't been allowed to see them. After almost crashing the car, they arrived at the bowling alley where their dad continued to be verbally abusive towards them and continued drink and showing openly drunk behaviour, throwing bowling balls around the alley, swinging around the bowling slide that little ones or people not so good at bowling use to help them roll the ball and when he took our youngest to the toilet where he proceeded to break the taps at the sink. Never in a million years did I expect to get a call from my kids screaming and crying down the phone at me because their dad had been picking on them all day and night in his drunken state. I knew something would happen but not this. They were in another town where they didn't even know anyone or know anywhere else to go. I called people to see if they could drive me to where they were so I could get my children and come home, and no one would help not even the person I was in a relationship with. So, I was left with no other choice but to tell my daughter to call the police. I stayed on the phone to her whilst she used her brother's phone to call them. I then instructed her to wait for him to bring her brothers back from the toilet and then get them to sit with her and her other brother. I then told her to go to the security guard who had already observed some of what had gone on and explain that they needed help and somewhere to wait until the police came. Which I think he did. When the police came the security guard let them know they were there and then the children went to go out and meet them but froze when they saw their dad sat on the stairs. I told her to gather her brothers and explain that they were going to all hold hands and then on the count of three they were going to run down the stairs straight to the police car. From all that they had told me had gone on I was able to gauge what level of drunk he was, so I knew he was in no position to see them get past. He spotted them at a time that was too late for him but a good time to a degree for them as they were already with the police. He went over to see what was going on, I was still on the phone. When he got to where they were he asked them what was going on my daughter told him that they wanted to go home

"Come on then" he said, "I'll take ya."

My daughter reminded him that he was drunk so he said for her to call a taxi and she told him she didn't know any taxi numbers. He was offering my daughter his phone for her to call a taxi when she shouted to him, she didn't want to use his phone because they weren't going home with him. He was confused and said "I thought you said you wanted to go home"

she said "yeah, we do but not with you"

He replied "oh so you wanna go home back to Reading"

My daughter said yes and that was it he went off on one

"Well fuck you then, fuck the lot of ya." He turned to my eldest son and said, "especially you you're not my son anymore you're nothing but a pussy."

They were all screaming and crying, my eldest went to go for Warren as he had attempted to go for my daughter and threw a bank card in her neck with enough force that she had a mark. The police put the kids in a taxi and sent them home to me. Over the following weeks the police came to our house to take statements and I was called by social services and told that because I am no longer with the father now and that because I reside in a different town that on this occasion they would leave the kids with me but I was not to let the children go with him again because if anything like this was to happen again then they would be removed from my care and neither of us would be able to see as it be considered that I am the one who put them in danger. I had to go to all my children's schools and explained what happened and put pictures of their dad and grandad up on their school files, so they knew not to let the children go with them. When I got to the younger two's primary school, which was also my place of work I had to do the same and also explain about the black eye that my middle son had which had to be logged and filed on all systems in and outside of the school. I also went to see a solicitor to see if there was anything that could be put in place to be told that actually his refusal to go on the boys birth certificates meant he had no rights over them any way and even though he was on my daughters certificate because of when she was born and the fact that we weren't married at the time meant he also didn't have any rights there either and that a lot of the things he was saying to the children is called emotional abuse so based on that alone I had the right to stop contact. So, this just reinforced the fact that when I had put a stop him seeing the children because of the distress he was causing with the things he said, I had the right to do so and was doing the right thing. Also, any time I had allowed him to see them again I was well within my rights not to let him whether it be by choice or manipulation but also that my children went through all of that for nothing, as had I of been heard instead of being painted as a bitter woman this is something my children would never have had to endure and all any one can say is sorry.

This didn't stop his games though giving sob stories to his friends on the rare occasion that he saw them but never giving all the facts even though he himself received a letter from social services telling him he is banned from having contact with his children until they are 18 because of his actions.

Overtime we got into a routine of being without him and life seemed a lot better, I was no longer going out, smoking, or drinking as I had given up after a year going mad with it to the point where it had affected my liver. I replaced all of this with religion as I took on the practicing of Islam. It wasn't hard as I was never bang on the drink like that and often had breaks and knew my limits. The hardest thing was giving up smoking as I found it even harder to sleep and my flashbacks seemed to be more prevalent. But me and my children enjoyed the exploration of the religion and trying out something new. The difficulty came from those who were not happy with our choices. The friends who had not wanted to go out whenever I did were suddenly going out and inviting me or turning up at my house with bottles of drink. My siblings on my dad's side and their mum decided they were no longer going to associate with me and decided that I must have been forced into it and reached out to the children to share their concerns. Apparently, everything was so awful, so awful in fact that no one bothered to report me or try to save the children. I was glad they distanced themselves from me anyway as they had no bearing or significance in our lives and even the kids will tell you all they did was take them to church and then get them to help cook. I respected they wanted to keep their relationship with our dad, but they couldn't accept that I didn't even after what he did. When I found out my sister was getting married, I saw that I was deemed as the troublemaker as I was only invited on the grounds that I didn't cause trouble with our older sister, even though this was never a thing we just agreed that we couldn't agree to disagree and so it was easier to just not speak. I even shopped where she worked, and she would just treat me as though as I was any other customer. The decider for me was that the children were going to be in separate rooms from the adults and their/our dad was going to be there. I just chose not to go and didn't say anything. It hadn't helped that I had heard from the man I was seeing that my sister was getting married about two weeks before she told me herself. He had heard it from my brother on my dad's side, they also told him that I had gone into Islam just to keep some man happy and how I was out of order coz I had the kids doing it too. I was not happy about this especially as they were saying it to the man I was seeing and that was the last thing I wanted him to think. At the time I felt he was different to the kid's dad, but the only real difference was he didn't hit me. So, another narcissist being told he had the power he wanted. Which was easy for me to say now as I couldn't fully see that then. I had even taken my Shahada without him knowing so it didn't become about him but, a lady saw him talking to me at the park after an Islamic talk I had gone to. She approached us and he said to her he was just asking me if I had enjoyed the talk and she told him that I must have as I had taken my shahada.

spread your wings, speak your truth, write it down & let it 151 go

He said to her that was good and then left. The woman told me that I should stay away from him because he was a funny guy and had found the separation from his wife difficult and all he ever did was talk about the breakup when he saw people. She felt too much time had passed for things to still be bothering enough for him to be stopping people he knew to talk about it. But I felt I had connected with him on an intellectual level.

CHAPTER 12

This last time I went out was to an over 30s function I felt it would be much better than just going out in town and would have better chance of meeting someone there and said to myself if I didn't then I would just leave things as they were as I it would then mean I was obviously meant to be alone. I never expected to get to know the taxi driver who took me home. He caught my eye in his rear-view mirror. He liked me because I was keeping myself to myself and wasn't being a typical drunk that he was used to picking up. After we talked for a while, he gave me his number and said it was up to me if I called him or not. I did and we spoke quite often and if he was available, he would pick me up or drop me off to where I was going. We spent a month or so just talking before he took me on a date, and we still just talked even after that before we became sexually intimate. With us both having problems with our exes we decided to keep our relationship quiet, so we didn't have any added aggravation. With him being the single parent to his kids our set up worked just fine he would sleep at his house, and I would sleep at mine, and we would both always put our kids first so if anything came up with them date night or chill nights whatever it was, we had planned would automatically be cancelled. As the children got older, they clocked on to the fact that I had a night visitor and called him the midnight monster because they never saw him. As they got even older, we got a little more open, but they never really officially met him. Things started to change when I got feelings for him and wanted to become more exclusive, he said he had thought about it but the first time he was going to tell someone he changed his mind because of an argument we had which ended in me launching CDs that I made for him at him. The next time he changed his mind was because when he asked me what I would do if he died. I told him I would mourn him for however long it took me and then move on. That was not what he wanted to hear as the women from his community would stay single and raise the children. But I told him he can't have that kind of wife loyalty when he doesn't

spread your wings, speak your truth, write it down & let it 153 go

have me in a wife situation. At this point I was not bothered by our situation, but we started to grow apart, and, in the end, it was just sex and arguments until I called it off. He had gone from telling me that I was too good for him to I'd never find anybody like him. Which seems ridiculous because when things aren't working out it clearly shows things weren't right so why would I want someone else like him anyway. He wasn't all he cracked up to be and I ended up having to teach him a lot of things including things about the religion which he claimed to be all about. He hadn't given any consideration to the fact that I might actually do my own research because I was genuinely interested in the religion he was just along for the ride. The relationship become draining after a while and other things were starting to get me down and I already struggled with recurring depression. Me and the kids had to be decanted due to neighboring properties subsiding, so we had to live in a different house for a year and a half. It was only meant to be a year at first, but time kept getting added on. Then my step aunty got sick with the sickle cell, and I was so close to her and so were my children, so we took that badly. I knew she was going to die as there was something different about her being ill this time. He never really supported me through this and just complained that I was different as I had changed. I didn't know what he had expected with all that had gone on but as far as he was concerned it wasn't his fault so why should he have to suffer. He even told me once that if I didn't change something then he would stop having sex with me. I told him that was fine which he wasn't expecting. He was like what, well I didn't expect you to say that I really thought saying that to you would work. I told him straight I'm doing my best and if that isn't good enough then what else does he expect me to do. Him saying odd things was quite a habit of his. When I was on medication one time, he said to me am I sure I was okay to have to sex as he didn't want to go ahead with it to then be accused of rape. I told him he shouldn't be having sex with someone at all if he feels that's even possible just because they're on medication. I was still functioning so still had my wits about me. Another time he asked me how come I wasn't scared of Warren and not him. What a question to ask, but I feel he only asked it because of another argument we had where he had become quite rude, and I retaliated. He then made a dig saying no one wonder Warren treated me like he did. I was lying in bed at the time and without even thinking I launched my cup that was full of drink at him. He came back into the room as he had made his digs as he was walking out and picked up a bottle of water and started asking me if I think I'm bad. That I wanna mind he doesn't do the same back to me and was threatening to squirt me with a bottle of water. He was taking too long so I got up and told him come then just do it if you're going to do it. He was taken aback and started telling me that I am crazy and asking if I thought I was some sort of man because I was squaring up to him. Whilst he was still stood there saying whatever he was saying I did the job for him and squirted the water on myself. With that he left and said I was crazy and no wonder I needed I therapy. At this point not only had I lost my step aunty I had also lost my nan who had died exactly a year and four days after my step aunty did.

Whilst my aunt's funeral was heart crushing my nans funeral had complex emotions around it. For many distinct reasons, firstly because we had been estranged for a year before my step aunty I had died. She had been staying with me again this time for an eye operation. The last time she had stayed was for a gall bladder operation. She wanted everyone to come together and chip in to pay for her operation and her being with me meant I had to see family that I didn't not want to see, worsened by the fact I had now learnt that another one had been a rapist during his teenage years and Levi used to keep watch whilst it was happening. They hadn't done anything to me but to me that was still beside the point. I let them have the meeting at my house and listened to them make all their excuses or say their reasons whichever one it was and then piped up and said "well someone needs to do somethings because it's my kids that are being kept awake at night whilst she's lying-in bed screaming in pain. As always, my step aunty who wasn't even my nans birth daughter stepped up again and had it covered. During this stay my nan had come to feel unwell and called for my step aunty to come and get her and that same night she had a heart attack.

We had become estranged because I had wanted her to meet my partner before she went as she had become very curious about who he was. I arranged for it to happen and then she changed her mind when he was on his way. When he arrived, I went up to her room to go and speak to her and give he the box of chocolates he had got for her. She started screaming and shouting I don't know who you're bringing in my room but get out of here. But I wasn't bringing anyone, that didn't stop her telling people that I did. She called her son and got him to her pick her up I got the kids up to say goodbye to her as I always did no matter how much she insulted me I always respected her. Levi came to collect her without saying a word and she left without saying a word and just left my kids sat there on the floor like nobodies. Then took to telling my step aunty that I only woke them so they could get money which was something I never did anyway. She had the same problem again with getting her kids to come together and pay for her operation and getting offended when they didn't it soon became apparent that her love language was money as she didn't even need anyone to pay for her eye operation as she had the money it was just a test to see who cared for her. My youngest sister was staying with us too, and they didn't see eye to eye. This was no secret, (pardon the pun) and my little sister was open about her feelings and openly asked our nan questions that she wanted answered that were difficult for my nan to face. Some of it I diffused because the kids were present mine and my sisters. And I also knew the answer to what she was asking as my nan had told me before that she was sorry as she had made lots of mistakes, but she was pleased with the person I had turned out to be. But I understood my sisters' frustrations as because of what had gone on it made it difficult for me and my sister to have a proper bond. We were always polite to each other but secretly my sister hated me or was angry with me. I never really knew this until my mum had died. Initially my sister had come to stay in Reading, but she stayed with our cousin until she decided to kick her out. So, she came to stay with me where I found out she was making mobile calls to a friend of hers so she could run up my phone bill so that I would have to give my share of my mum's compensation money to the phone company rather than get any beneficial use out of it. She had also been tormenting my daughter at night by making her scared of the giant teddy she had in her room she had won it at a fete in Twyford. My sister was telling her it was watching

spread your wings, speak your truth, write it down & let it 156 go

her, she also tried to encourage my daughter to run away. I knew my sister wasn't happy with me when she got to mine as she said to me why can't I just act like myself, which is hard to do when you don't know who you are. Plus, I felt out of sorts anyway and couldn't hear in one ear for about two weeks after the funeral. But didn't know she hated me enough to do things like that. I don't even know what I had done to her for her to be this way. I told her she had to leave, and she went to go and stay with another sister she had the friend who had been my neighbour in the flats. Her sister had called me and asked why I didn't talk through things with her, but I did, and she had been told I hadn't. she then went on to say I shouldn't have kicked her out at night as she could have been raped by the guys outside or anything. I felt like this was just an emotional dig to get me to take her back and even more so when her sister said to me, she wouldn't be letting an 18-year-old make her feel threatened. I wasn't feeling threatened I was angry and did what I had to do to protect my daughter, when I looked back on this later it made me chuckle as she was the one who was struggling to confront her for stealing from her house and just decided to hide her things instead when she came to visit. Obviously, it's her choice but I found it a bit contradictory. This time round things were different, and it was my nan that was causing the problems this time even before she left that night. Shouting screaming and kicking off, slamming doors. I called one of my step uncles, he spoke to her and that made her even more angry, and she told me she would remember that I called my uncle for her.

All of these circumstances hadn't helped. I spoke to her for a year before my step aunty died and when my step aunty did die, she came over but didn't stay with us she just came to visit. When my nan died, I was in therapy and had made a lot of realisations like my nan having to have seen the pattern of how here kids were and therefore being able to have seen the same behaviour traits in others like my dad. I had also become unsure about how I felt about my nan as I thought I loved her but for years she kept me in dreadful situations with having to have unwanted family members in my house and around my children. Especially one day when she invited one round and had fallen asleep leaving my daughter to answer the door to him, I have never got home so quickly in all my life. When I blasted through the door, he was sat on the far side of my sofa by the wall and my daughter who I had stayed on the phone to was upstairs in her room with the door shut. My nan dying meant I would never have to be in either of these situations ever again. I had to decide whether I was going to go to the funeral in Grenada or not. The cons of going were so big it hardly seemed worth the risk. As I didn't know if her sons Ashbert and Tony were going to be there. Tony was less likely to be there as he was still in hiding from the rest of us. And when my nan was told about his whereabouts she wasn't interested. She went into herself and didn't want to speak to anybody. I guess there's not a lot to say when you find out your daughter has known that your son has been in hiding for years and had been in touch with him and fully aware of his whereabouts and letting on in any way whatsoever when you're wondering how he is and if he's dead or alive. My aunt was too stubborn to come and see my nan at my house so she just sent Tony's girlfriend round with their kids so my nan could see her grandchildren that she hadn't seen for countless years. I had already faced Ashbert at my mum's funeral but this it was going to be different as we would all have been staying in the same house. Not only that after my mum's funeral Ashbert spoke to my nan on the phone. She wanted to confront him about the letter I had found from my mum to him, and she was asking him why he did the things he did, and he was telling her it was her fault. That made me angry, and I took the phone and told him he shouldn't blame her for what he did as he should be able to take responsibility for his own actions. He told me that I should just shut up and asked who I thought I was talking to because I wasn't any better because I was a dangerous person and always had been.

That right there is why trying to talk to people for closure is a myth as if the person hasn't changed, they will be dismissive, the other predicament is the manipulation when they tell you all the right things but still also haven't changed, they just change the way they go about doing things to still get what they want. Closure is found internally, and therefore forgiveness does not have to be outwardly given. When you say to people like this that they are forgiven they hear 'I am open to you for you to mistreat me again'.

Some people at work were quite supportive and one in particular thought this was a good moment to tell me how brave I was once I had made the decision to go but I didn't want or need to hear that then, I wasn't good at accepting kindness at the best of times. I explained the situation to my boss and booked a week off. My partner at the time wasn't very helpful and refused to take me to the airport until I told him my brother was going to get up and get the bus to come with me. And his last words to me before I went up the stairs to the airport where you drop people off, he looked at me and said you look ugly when you cry. He knew what I was going to be facing and this is what came of his mouth. When I got to Grenada, I was picked up by Levi, but I kept quiet and spoke when I was spoken to. The next day we went to make the funeral arrangements but were told they couldn't go ahead with such short notice but after explaining that we had travelled to be here and some of us were due back by the end of the week, they pulled their fingers out and got it sorted. I helped to choose the coffin which was brown with white material inside it and my cousin, Levi's daughter chose her outfit as she knew what our nans favourite church outfit was. We had the funeral the next day I was holding it together well until they played a song, she used to sing which I think is called come thou art. The day after we spent a short amount of time at the beach and that same night I flew back to England. My nan did think a lot of me but so much was done in the wrong way. I think I had got caught up in the fear of who was going to be there and falling out with Selina hadn't helped. She had let me down at the last minute she had agreed to help my brother out with the kids so he could still go to work. She came to meet me at the school so that I could introduce her to the teachers so she could pick them up from school without any problems. She was happy to pick them up and bring them home and cook and clean and then she would go home when my brother got in so she could see to her dog. Plans changed as it turned out her dog had been reported stolen and once, she saw that she contacted the owners to give the dog back as she hadn't known it was stolen. The agreement then was for her to come and stay and the whole point in her helping out was that my daughter was not under any pressure as she had exams around this same time, which she managed to so well in despite the circumstances. But then Selina's brother brought her a new dog which she agreed to leave with him until I got back but then changed her mind and said she couldn't wait any longer and started to ask if she could just bring the dog with her which I wasn't having, and neither was my brother as he doesn't like dogs. I couldn't believe that these were the conversations she was having with all I had going on. I seriously very rarely asked her or anyone for anything and when I did need help and asked it was important. I lost my patience in the end and told her to forget it and to not speak to me again.

When I got back my middle son had SATs, I had a call because we were running late that morning but initially, they had planned to call my brother thinking that I wasn't in the country. Another member of staff told them that I was back just not coming in. I dropped my son off and went home as the plan was to have the day to myself which in the end I didn't even get to do as my daughter had a dentist appointment. When I went back into work on the Tuesday the deputy, head was sent to ask me why I hadn't come in on the Monday. I couldn't actually believe I was being asked this and my exact response was

"Oh my god, are you actually being serious I can't believe this. I have spent from the ages 8 up until 15 being raped and sexually abused by members of family, to then lose my aunty and now lose my nan and now had to contemplate whether I was going to see the uncles who were the ones who had raped and abused me at her funeral because they are her children. I flew out on the Monday landed Tuesday had the funeral Wednesday and flew back on the Thursday waited 7 hours in Antigua airport for the next flight home flew in on the Friday and have been with my kids all weekend is it too much to ask that I would want a day to myself?"

He said he was so sorry, but he had been sent to ask which baffled me because why would you send someone to ask that when you knew what I was dealing with before I left. He went back to the head's office, and I went back into class to the finish the school day and help send the children off. On my way out I went to the headteacher's office. She asked if I was ok, and I replied that I was and had come to see if the Deputy Head was as, it was a lot to take in as it is and the way I unleashed it all could not have helped. The headteacher said she was concerned because of my response as it was just a question and I told her that was just the answer because it was. As if I wasn't going through enough, she then decided to report me for neglect as she had decided that more was going on than I was telling her. But it was what it was and what more did she need to be wrong because to me that was more than enough. The worse thing was we had already had a visit from a family worker, and she was happy to close our case considering everything that was going on. Obviously with having Complex Post Traumatic Stress Disorder, a mood disorder and Fibromyalgia and then having to deal with possibly having to see the people who were responsible for traumatising me what more did she need. I know she hadn't liked my decision to convert and so this seemed as if this was perfect opportunity for her to create something. My relationship wasn't great, but it wasn't bad in a way that I feel like she was implying. To a degree his mindset was similar to Warrens but he never hit me which obviously is a good thing but that did not mean his emotional treatment was any better. One great thing he did do for me was to take me to have some screaming therapy. We drove to the middle of nowhere and just stood there and screamed. I was really self-conscious at first, so he started it then I joined in and then he let me do it by myself. It was a great experience it felt like I had emptied and internal bucket and then just had to deal with the empty space it left. It was also thanks to him that I did my driving lessons. He found me a good, priced instructor and also supported me through when I struggled. Getting this done also meant that he didn't have to do all the driving.

It became clear that we had reached a stagnant point in our relationship and the whole thing just seemed like one big joke in the end. But my children were not being neglected and had she of wanted to look at what might be up with them then maybe she and some others should have been taking a look in a mirror because it was thanks to them and all of their services that my children were able to be retraumatised by their dad again.

Bob, this is the nickname we gave him for when he wasn't around, no particular reason it was just a random thing that my brother made up on the spot one day and so we just went with it, couldn't come to terms with the fact that I'd rather be alone than with him. He tried everything he begged, brought gifts one time he even cried down the phone to me which made me laugh and he was soon laughing with me asking why I was laughing so as I had suspected he was putting on to get to me. Just to put it out there I would never laugh at a man who was genuinely crying as I think it is healthy and it's about time, we. Lived in a world where men are allowed to express their emotions and to be able to do it comfortably. He then drew it back to sex, but he had stopped being able to meet my needs once I had gained more emotional growth as he was longer able to connect with me. That's when I realised enough was enough and the relationship was dead in the water and called it a day and have been single ever since.

So, the same week I was back from Grenada I was having to deal with that too. My house wasn't tidy when they came and the kids' rooms were a mess but again, I don't know what more they expected I had just got back from all of that. The family worker was concerned as to why the school was doing this to me as I was their colleague the only answer I had was that my boss was doing things she shouldn't be doing with people she shouldn't be doing it with and she was unsure as to whether I knew or I had been with him myself, so she was exerting her power by using her position of authority. My fibromyalgia was getting worse no doubt because of stress. I was always more prone to flare ups in the cold weather but now it was happening more often. Every morning I was waking up tired well that's if you could call it waking up as I never really slept. I would always feel sick and have no appetite it was like I was forcing my body to do more than it could manage at that time of the day and throughout. It meant that the kids were late some mornings, and this wasn't helped by my youngest who also struggled to manage in the mornings as he also struggled with sleep, he has now been diagnosed with Autism and has been kept on the waiting list to be seen about whether or not he has ADHD, even if I was on his case which some mornings, I didn't have the energy to do as I could barely speak for heaving we would still be late. So, I would just be upsetting him for no reason, already suspecting he had autism being on his case like that, over things that neither of us has control over made me feel bad, so I stopped.

CHAPTER 13

Being diagnosed with fibromyalgia was a bit of a relief at first as it explained why I had so many complications and made sense as to why I had days when I couldn't move especially when I had period pains and why my depression felt different sometimes as Fibromyalgia brings its own depression. This doesn't come though until you feel more of the symptoms coming through and you gradually stop being able to do more of the things that you were able to do. On some occasions in a bid to not let the fibromyalgia take over your life you try to do some things still anyway knowing that you will have to pay for it after, with pains and cramps and brain fog and all the other many symptoms that come with it. Some days you can struggle through the pain, some days the pain is so bad it makes you feel nauseous. On the worst days I can barely make it from my bed to the bathroom. Sometimes resting helps and sometimes it just hurts anyway.

I would get to work and throw myself into what I had to do no matter how much I was struggling unless it was to the point of not being able to move from my bed. They set up a time keeping sheet and made me report to my team leader each time I came in. I felt patronized but still got on with it, my boss said it was to help me, so they were going to build a case for me to go to the occupational therapist, but it was to help me. I wasn't sure I believed this but got on with it as they were gonna do what they wanted to do anyway. I wrote up my own piece to go with it and when I gave it to my boss again, she reassured me that this was in my best interest. This didn't make the process any less stressful as everything was in theirs and my fibro's hands.

I got called in to the occupational therapy appointment in town which I was not best pleased about after the appointment because I bumped into my dad on the way back to my car. This was actually my car now

spread your wings, speak your truth, write it down & let it 164
go

that I had been able to get as a result of my step aunty leaving me some money when she died. Another trigger for my CPTSD as if I wasn't under enough stress from work alone. The occupational therapist was really nice and after looking at all my other medical information she looked me asked "do you not value your mental health?" I told her I did but didn't know what else to do because look how they are treating me as a colleague I have a son who still goes to the school so imagine what they would be like if I was just a parent. She agreed as my boss had added in the report that I had a son that goes to the school and that my lateness was having an impact on him. So, the OT deemed this as a personal vendetta. It was quite funny because my Psychodynamic therapist also felt the same, she had concluded that my boss actually felt threatened by me as she could not read me. Once the OT had read through all my doctors' letters and notes she decided it was best to slam the disability discrimination act on them. I walked into work the next day passing my boss and my team leader who both never uttered a single word to me not even a breath.

Whilst I still struggled, I continued to work and even resorted to trying medication so I could still attend everyday but then the medication started to get the best of me and some days I ended up either not going in or being later than usual because of how messed up the meds had me. 10 different meds later it was decided that meds were not for me and that I was to continue as best as I could and listen to my body. Which is easier said than done when you've got work on your case watching your every move whilst also telling you how great you are at your job and then treating you like you're not, then calling on you when they need you going back to telling you how good you are then back to treating like you're not after they have done everything to scrutinise you from the inside out. It also didn't help that I was put back down the lower end of the school to work with the younger ones who although I enjoyed working with took a lot of cleaning up after which meant I was more likely to pick up illness and that's exactly what happened. This meant my level of flare ups increased, in the end I got so ill that I couldn't shake it off and struggled to recover fully. Every time I felt okay enough to go back in, I ended up getting sent home.

The new boss was no different, my old boss had become the CEO of the schools. My new boss had me up under the ill health review act not long after being there and had me signing in again so they could keep an eye on the time I was in so they could have it for their meetings. This soon became a thing for everybody. The meeting was so formal, and I knew my job was at risk and there were other people in the meeting who I didn't know. As soon as the meeting started, I had to get out as I felt like I was suffocating. A colleague who had kindly sat in the meeting with me calmed me down and we went back in. They used the times as I knew they would and even used a time that they knew I was helping out with a safeguarding situation, with someone one of my sons knew. I still kept going despite the stress I was feeling, and they still had me in doing my one-to-one role although it couldn't be called that because it was for 6 different children in two different classes. I enjoyed my role, but it was made difficult when you suggest things that you know would help the child, you're with and things don't get done. Then you get accused of being too personally involved. maybe I was on some occasions, and I know I did definitely get attached to the last one to one role that I had before this one, but you would have had to not of had a heart not too. but things not getting done when they were in the child's best interests and would be a benefit to all made doing the job very difficult. What was the point in being good at it if none of the right things were supported? The child's interests weren't ever at the forefront of the school it was all about politics and money. It was almost like being a kid again, being shut down and unheard and everything being done against me. On the plus side of being good at my job I knew I had made some positive impact on them even if it only lasted whilst they were at school.

I soon found myself in another OT appointment where it was decided it was best to get me out of there as soon as possible before they got rid of me and left me without pay. Having been in hospital twice at this point because of chest pains it was decided that this wasn't a risk I should be willing to take, and my doctors said that really, I should be taking these chest pains as sign to reevaluate my work situation. Particularly as the symptoms for what I was having are the same as a heart attack. It was due to severe Costochondritis which is another symptom of Fibromyalgia. Whenever it gets that bad to the point where my arm goes numb then I must call an ambulance and be taken to the hospital for tests as that would be the only way to determine whether I have had a heart attack or not. I was signed off on a long-term basis about six months before the lockdown started. My time was spent waking my boys for school, doing little bits of housework in between resting. Like literally washing a couple of plates, then resting, get up again to sweep the floor then rest and so on and so on. It wasn't helped by the fact that my back pain was really playing up. It was unusually tender to the point where I felt like my lower body was going to collapse underneath me. I also had a few weeks of hydrotherapy which helped with the fibromyalgia, it's so much easier to move in the water and helped that the water was warm. On days I had a little extra strength I wrote poetry.

My final ill health work meeting was done via Teams as it was during lockdown, we discussed my options, but I already knew what they were as I had discussed them with my OT and with the person who I had my ill heath pension meeting with. This meant I was prepared for the final meeting and so had already made a decision. This didn't sit well with my boss, and she ended the meeting by saying that I had wanted this to happen, which I thought was quite rude considering I was only in this position because she put me in it in the first place. Everything was at her detriment so had she of accepted my circumstances for what they were and left me to do what she herself even said I was good at then it would never have come to what it did. The sad thing now is I can't even say that I really one hundred percent miss my job because the end goal was never the same for everyone. I miss the children and seeing the difference I made in their lives just even being at the workplace. But I don't miss the struggle and pain of seeing the children where a bigger difference needs to be made and it not getting done. Hearing that we were not here to babysit, or we are only here to teach to me is not a sufficient excuse, especially when it is known that you cannot educate a traumatised mind. The entanglements in the mind need to be dealt with and freed before there can be room for the child or anyone for that matter to be able to engage in education of any kind. When you know how to make that difference and you have the skills to do it but the people with bigger titles that hold the key to finances do not want those needs to be met because they are seen as an inconvenience it becomes more than frustrating it becomes heartbreaking. Even more so when you know they can see it too, you can't say you want the best for a child and then not deliver what is best for them.

I know schools are changing now and working from a trauma based approached, if done properly this will make such a difference. I also think that needs to be available to the parents. As many of them will have unresolved trauma too which will influence their children and teachers and other staffing members need the help too as they have things that have go on in their lives that have an impact on who and how they teach. It doesn't make sense to think otherwise when teaching staff spend an ample amount of time with our children. We should also make ourselves aware of the fact the children know when a teacher is a good teacher. Until we can accept that a lot more goes into teaching than just teaching things will never change for the better.

My contract came to a proper end in June 2020, and I had been off for six months before this so lockdown was already my normal. The only thing that changed for me was the children now being home all the time. It was hard to get into a routine of homeschooling. The children struggled with the change of having to do schoolwork at home. Not having the same background knowledge as teachers in some subjects made the schooling take longer than it would have in school as research had to be done in order to obtain the knowledge to be able to teach at home. Then you had the issue of some teachers not being happy with the outcome or level of work so some had to be redone. Then there was the issue of some teachers not fully understanding the use of the school apps and technology and the complaining about the children not doing what needed to be done. I have noticed that this apparent in the school as well and then they wonder why some children do not behave as they want them to. I believe it's important for teachers to remember that whilst they are consciously teaching their lesson, they are also unconsciously teaching our children how they behave as people so shouldn't be surprised when the children are the same.

This blurred the lines between school and home life. But still we struggled through. It was a bit easier when teachers taught throughout the day via devices, once they could see the struggle it felt like that any work that was set for lessons teachers weren't available for was more manageable.

When we weren't stressing about schoolwork we watched movies together, had plenty of banter, long deep talks, and time alone in our rooms. During my time alone when I wasn't writing I was thinking and going over things that arose in my mind as they came up. Some good memories would pop up and some bad. But I let them be and let the processing take place making notes or sometimes just being. I did get stressed a few times as my friend Selina who I chose to reconnect with after hearing her mum was ill. At first it was awkward and then it became okay with her sometimes feeling the need to bring up when we weren't speaking. She went through some things, but her mum had been there for her. The strain in friendship started to come back and was made even more apparent during the lockdown when she rang me every day and wanted to be on the phone all the time. I was struggling to manage homeschooling, constantly being in, helping my children cope with the same feeling and their other emotional needs and get things done that I wanted to do and have time to myself. I told her in the end, and we had a bit of break only being in touch every few days. Not to say she is a bad person as she has her own struggles too, but it doesn't help.

Now having a bit of freer time to myself I was able to then sit with the conversation that myself and my brother had had in December 2019. He spoke the words to me of something that I had already considered myself but still wasn't really accepting seemed to hit different once he had made the same conclusion and shared it with me. This also meant that I could not sit in the denial any longer. I had done it I had broken my family pattern. It had taken a while and had had some detrimental effects, but it had been done. I had kept my children from enduring any direct damage from any of my family members especially the ones who were the culprits of inflicting rape and sexual abuse onto others within and outside of the family. Whilst I was not able to protect them from growing up in a household where there was domestic violence which could have only been done if the tools I have now I had then. Others before me would have had to of been healed for that to have been possible. However, even that I have grown from as I was able to get out of that and acquire the help that was required to get out and stay out. Although I did have a momentary lapse when I made contact with Warren to get him to help support our daughter when she was getting mixed up in things that weren't good to the point that I had to ask her to leave home due to the safeguarding issues it was creating for her younger siblings, not just by associating with certain people but by also bringing them to our home and then I began to receive letters about other serious things she had been doing. He became more of a hinderance than a help which I should have known really but I was stuck with nowhere else to turn and let others convince me that because he was her dad, I should get him to help as she is 18 now. It didn't take much time before he reminded me of who he was as a person when his foul mouth started and the insults started coming through, this got even worse after I had my first poetry book self-published. Mainly because he didn't like the bits in it that he knew signified him and the ones I wrote to my children apologizing to them that I had not been able to pick a man who was able to be a good father. In the end he was no help just like many others around me and now because of that me and my daughter have grown further apart. So now sadly she has not been able to see my growth as a woman and see that I now see the strength of which I now see I hold within myself. Or the benefits of knowing and living with in your power for the good of yourself and not for what others perceive to be good. Having the right people around your children is so important. No one will love them like you do and no one will parent them like you do. If they think you are doing things wrong, they should take the time out to help you instead of helping your child become more distant from you just because they believe the things your child is doing is okay because apparently, it's normal which everyone has their own perception of. Things like oh that's what all children do at that age or well they are old enough to do that now are not acceptable reason to let your children do things. Legally ready doesn't mean emotionally ready and everybody doing it doesn't make it right. Another one is saying you should let it happens because it's the same as something you did, that doesn't make it okay either and when your child is not living through the same experiences as you are then surely the outcome of their life should be different from yours but in a better way. No one will parent your child like you do as they will never deeply have the same want for your child, and no one has the right to tell your child your history especially if they are not going to accompany it with good advice. My whole life has been filled and surrounded with toxic people both male and female. I never wish I could go back to change things as all that has happened has been enforced upon me by others so things would have always of been the same. Instead, what I do is embrace myself and the changes that I have made to be able to become better so that my natural path of negativity is derailed by the path I have chosen to take of positivity. I have now dug deep enough to begin to find out who I am and who I have always been underneath the mounted layers of trauma that disrupted me being able to see me.

Looking back on it all I guess the broken relationship with my daughter was inevitable, not just because of my trauma as healing from that would have helped to at least salvage something. But more due to the fact that my parenting has been completely undermined from the get-go when it came to my daughter, and it continued on into her adult life. It has now materialised that the more I noticed and pulled people up on what they did the quieter they became about what they were doing. As I sit here, I can actually think of a list of what undermining has been done.

So, there was the not being allowed to cream her skin.

Then when she was about a year old and with Janine for the weekend Janine took her to get her haircut without my permission. When I expressed my unhappiness towards what she had done, J told me I was overreacting and it was only a little bit, so it didn't matter.

Then there was the time when Janine took her from my house without me knowing. It was my son's birthday party and at first Janine had asked if she could take my daughter to which I said no. It's her brother's birthday why would I want her to be away from her brother. birthdays are something that you celebrate as a family especially whilst you're growing up. Janine said that was why she should go with her because it was her brother's birthday so the day should be all about him. But it still was with his siter there by his side just like he had been for her birthday. The children were playing in the garden, and I had gone into the kitchen and that's when Janine took her chance and left with my daughter. When I called her, she answered and said she would bring her back the next day, but she never did. Not having any things for her they brought her some clothes I then later found out that she wasn't even with J she was in with Janine's daughter Aimee keeping her company in her new house. I sent Janine a message telling her out of order she was and that my daughter was my daughter, and she had no right to do this. Janine responded by saying that my daughter needed a break as a break would be good for her as it wasn't fair for her to be in the house with her brothers all the time. I told Janine that was stupid as her brothers are a part of her life and so they should grow up together. Having siblings is a part of my daughter's life. She then got mad and had the cheek to call Warren the same man that she hated for beating me and cried down the phone to him asking him what was wrong with me as she didn't know why I was treating her as though she had kidnapped my daughter. Which really is basically what she had done even I never said that to her.

As my daughter got older, she would complain to them if she was unhappy about something I had said or stopped her from doing and they would comfort her and feed into what she had said and later this transformed into them moaning about me with her and telling her things about my past that she did not need to hear from them. I told my children what they needed to know in a way that was appropriate for their ages when they asked. And telling my daughter that I treated her as badly as my mum treated me which was not in the slightest bit true. My daughter never got beat for eating food, she was never underfed and was never made to lie to anyone about who she was to me, and I never sent her off with anyone knowing they were rapists. I did punish with hitting for a while on some occasions, when I saw this made no difference and just made her scared of me which was never my intention I stopped. That didn't stop her being angry with me though as she hated that I still wouldn't let her do certain things like having sleepovers at the houses of people I do not or have not even met. And had Janine of been the friend to my mum that she had claimed she had been then she would have known this, and it would have done Janine some good to have taken a look in the mirror because I don't see where she has been much better than my mum ever was.

Everything became all about my daughter and whenever I mentioned about the boys everything was always alright. Oh, they are fine, oh we can't always have them all, sometimes it's good to let your daughter come on her own. It was amazing how I was only deemed to be a bad parent when it came to my daughter. They loved to buy her gifts all the time too and very rarely for the boys. I told them to stop as it wasn't fair, when they said they couldn't afford to buy for all I told them in that case not to buy for any.

CHAPTER 14

The worst of it came when I found Islam, I had spoken to my children about making the changes and most of their friends are Muslim so if anything, they knew more than me. From their child like understanding they were happy with having a double celebration of two Eid's as long as I still cooked Christmas dinners on Christmas day. So, I agreed and together we embraced the new changes and routines and broadened our minds with knowledge. At this time, the children were still seeing their dad so I was more than happy for him to have the children for Christmas as we would not be doing anything but that never ended happening due to his lack of commitment with parenting and his alcoholic and abusive behaviour towards the children, which I wrote about earlier.

When Janine had found out that we had made this change she asked if the children could go to her if they were not going with their dad. I said I would ask the children and see what they wanted to do. This was not something they wanted to do as it meant them staying and they didn't want to do that. When I relayed this information back to her she was not impressed. The children were happy to go for the present, but they were not a fan of her cooking and didn't want to sleep there. I told her the children were happy to come but wanted to come back home and she didn't want to do it that way because she wanted to have a drink at Christmas so wouldn't be able to drive, so the children decided not to go. When I gave the news to Janine once again, she proceeded to tell me that I was out of order and being unfair to the kids and it was up to me if I wanted to make this choice, but I didn't have to make the kids suffer as well. I continued to stand my ground, and this led to an argument where I ended up unleashing to her all the things that she had done that were out of order and that she had no right to do. Not liking the truth, she went and told my friend who I had met in the flat when I moved from care. My friend called me and said that Janine was really upset and said I shouldn't have said some of the things I said to her as they were hurtful. When I asked if Janine had told her everything, she had to me for I responded to her with those things and surprise, surprise no she hadn't. Janine had gone crying to one of my step uncles. He called and expressed his concerns I explained myself to him and that was left at that.

No one even knew why Janine was playing such a big role in our family or why she continued it long after falling out with my mum and my mum dying. Even before my step aunty died, she had expressed the same concerns. Me and Janine kept our distance for a while after that and we are distant again now as again her and her daughter were undermining me behind my back again telling my daughter more and more things about my past without any real substance and not highlighting the fact that I had been making changes to my life for the better. But well really what I could expect as that's not what they were seeing or wanted to see. They used my past behaviors to excuse my daughter's behavior and choices and told her I had no right to stop her from the things she was doing because I hadn't been any better myself but that was exactly why I wanted better for my daughter. Instead, she found comfort in those who supported her unhealthy choices that could have just been put down as mistakes instead of becoming her lifestyle. Just because they thought it was okay and suited them and keeping her happy meant she would always be happy to do things for them. Since then, my daughter made the choice to stop living with her dad and she has been living with these very same people. The sad thing is when they look back on their lives, they are not happy with some of the things they have done so I don't know why they would encourage others to act in the same way.

Just as I was becoming more acquainted with sitting in my power I endured another bombshell, which left me in quite a confused state as worst-case scenario was death. Lots of women have this procedure done but I'm sure it's not any less scary whether you have a trauma brain or not. Which I will have for the rest of my life now, now that I know this, I know that I always have to think through my first thought as

I will forever engage in flight, fight, or freeze mode as a first response. But still as an overthinker everything has to be thought through in great detail. So having a smear test to be told you have HPV so bad that your cervix is in a terrible state to the point where it needs to be operated on to be removed as it is on the verge of being cancer if it isn't already, is absolutely awful. And it was so bad that they were not going to be able to tell if it was Cancer or not until after that removed all that need removing. It turns out this is why back pain had been so bad to the point where that crumbling feeling was bringing me to tears and I was struggling to walk from my bed to the wardrobe let alone anywhere else. It also explained my unusually large outbreak of Hidradenitis Suppurativa which is a painful skin condition that causes abscesses. They say it is strongly associated with obesity which I am now considered to be, yet I have had this since I was a size 12 but back then I didn't have a proper diagnosis. Either way it is a lifelong condition.

Being one who needs answers I looked for some which I always do before I can accept that there aren't any there or they are not meant to be found in that moment. I found that HPV cannot be pinpointed to any one person, anyone can get it and you can even get it if you and your partner have stayed loyal to each other and been the only people each other have been with. This set up a whole new thought process as to whose fault it could have been that this had happened. Was it because of the rapes, was it because of any of my exes who cheated, was it someone who I had unprotected sex with when I didn't love myself enough to respect my body? at this point I was glad that I was not having sex with anyone as I had decided that celibacy was what I needed, and it has definitely helped so I am glad that I found the strength to do it. After my hospital appointment where they told me my cervix was in such a state and due to my prominent level of sensitivity and where one of the nurses found it highly amusing that I hadn't sex for three years. I had to put plans in place for what was going to happen around the time of my operation and leading up to it especially knowing it was going to cause a fibro flare and being sensitive to medication I knew it was going to have a longer lasting effect on me. Again, I turned to my friend Selina who basically decided she couldn't be there for me because she was to upset over a fall out, she had with a longtime friend. I had been supporting her through the process of the fall whilst also talking to her about what was going on with me as she was aware of it before the fall out with her friend. She promised she would come over when she got back from the break at her friends, I thought this would be good for us as we clearly needed each other with what we were both going through. Instead of coming to see me, she decided to stay home and do her washing and get her nails done. We talked it through when she then opened up and said that she found it too upsetting which I get but didn't have time for. I needed to find someone who was going to support my boys at least if not me. But she was unable to put her feelings aside to be there saying that no one is ever there for her when she needs them. I asked her to name a time I wasn't there for her when she was in need and knowing I have always been there for her throughout our friendship she could not name a time I wasn't. So, with that our friendship ended again, she said she thought I would understand, and I did and so left her with me understanding her does not mean that I have to invalidate myself. Which is true and the point stands even truer when you watch the same person help others to the point where she can't cope and gets no thanks and listen to them complain to you about the people they are helping. I do get that you can be so close to someone that it hurts when they go through things but sometimes you have to set that aside and if you can't then you cannot expect the same in return. When I think back to the times when I couldn't even share positive things with her it seems as though she has taken some of the stances she has as a way of punishing me for who I am and what I have got through in my life. Whilst I can see the twisted admiration or envy, I don't see the need for it as I believe she is just as capable.

Tessa had been in touch again and between her and my brother meals were prepared, cooked, and delivered. I also had additional support from my middles sons' coaches with lifts and talking support and the odd shopping drop off and my middles sons' friends mum brought me home from the hospital. My sons were such a major help but with older two knowing that the possible outcome was they had a lot on their minds. My eldest son came to me and said that he had it all clear in his mind that that if the diagnosis comes back as cancerous then he would have to step up and help my brother look after the boys as there is no one else to help them. My middle son came to me on separate occasion saying that he hopes I don't die because if I die then they really won't have anyone. My youngest knew I was going to have an operation, but he didn't know the detailed extent of the reason why.

The day I went in concerns were expressed again as they discussed the procedure saying it was like scooping out ice cream with an ice cream scoop. But they hadn't seen a cervix as bad as mine for a while and so they could not see the extent of what they were dealing with and would not be able to know that until I went down for the operation, so there was a possibility they would have to remove all of it as they were already having to take away a lot of it.

A bit of pressure lifted after the operation, and I was home the same day with all they had pumped my body with It was a good few days before I felt any affect from my fibromyalgia. The boys rallied round and kept me fed and watered. Their friends came to visit, and Tessa's sons came to see me too.

Whilst I know it is possible to live with cancer and recover from it there is something to be said about facing the possibility of something that could take your life away when you have contemplated taking your own life so many times. It brings such a different feeling, and you realize that at those times death seemed to be the only way to be free of the life you have had and the things in your mind that you have had to live with. Self-harming can sometimes be a temporary release as it feels as though it transforms your pain from one place to another and releasing it. But the scars leave a constant reminder of where you once were which leads to the thoughts of what you once endured. I started to feel that I had accomplished some of what I would have liked to have done as I now had three self-published poetry books one of which I was able to succumb enough confidence for to go on a photoshoot and use my own photo as the front cover. I had also won a business competition to get business support from my housing association to build a business and I

spread your wings, speak your truth, write it down & let it 178 go

had been on a few radio interviews at my local radio station BBC Radio Berkshire. And I had managed to start to heal and to grow. My friend who had done the photoshoot said not to think like that, but I felt like I needed to reassure myself that I had lived some life worth living for myself and my children, so it was okay to die if that's what was coming. It would have been a shame though because really, I have only just started to live and now, I had been cleansed of the horrors inside me, sexually, emotionally, physically, and spiritually.

I didn't let what was going on get the best of me which was another sign of how far I had come and getting the all clear was a sign that I was being freed to continue on in my newfound life. And that is what I have been doing ever since. I changed my Instagram profile to a poetry and quote page where I share all of my own writing work. I also have a Facebook page where I share the same things. I took to the idea of printing my own quotes on to bags and T-shirts and printing them into box frames. I had hoped to do mugs but did not realize that a different printer was needed to make this possible so that is my next aim. I also so have many flourishing ideas that I am yet to put into action but everything that I have been able to scrimp and save to do so far is available on my website. It is available to order from at any time of day or night and some things I make take at least 24 hours to set as some of the things I make are made with resin. I like to do it as it keeps my mind busy, it's easy to do and because it's all done online, I can do it all around my fibromyalgia which is better for me because it acts up when it feels like it. However, my main aim has been to help myself heal whilst sharing with others via my writing in the hope of helping them. Some people have reached out to me on social media after reading or listening to my work as on a few occasions I have recorded videos of myself reading my poetry. Now that I am living in more peace, I feel ready to open up more and keep going forward. I do get concerned sometimes about what others will do or say about my truth and the things I have shared about them from what they have done to me, and I think that will always be in me but now I am not going to let that stop me. I choose to no longer live-in fear of those who cannot speak the truth. I have also come to adapt my thinking when it comes to having a good time, after being in so much pain we fear having a good time in case it gets ruined. But trusting the experience is a good thing because there is always a solution no matter how hard the actions of the solution may be. Also, if more bad than good is happening then the situation just isn't good, so you're not meant to be in it. Having good times helps to keep you balanced so you're more likely to be able to cope with any difficult things that come along.

As part of my healing journey, I obtained my care notes and police reports and some of the things it has revealed has been shocking. Some of it I already knew Some I had already guessed so it had just been confirmed and some exposed where I had been majorly let down at what could have been turning points in my life. Having them has filled some blanks but not all and trying to remember the blanks is very draining and upsetting because nothing comes through. I am in a place now where I can leave them be knowing the blanks will be filled if and when they need to be. The most frustrating blanks are the ones in my file as those I will never see.

Like the school I attended in Maidenhead had they followed the correct protocol for when they were told things like I was telling them. It appears the process of schools still letting children down continues. Another was being blamed for my sexualised behavior that I was unaware of as a child, but this was the reason why I was never placed in any foster homes and some things I have not been able to see as they have been blacked out beyond the point of being able to read so somethings, I'll never know but I'm okay with that. I have had a lot of people to forgive so I can move forward. Some believe I haven't forgiven them because I do not speak to them, but I do not need to

spread your wings, speak your truth, write it down & let it go because my forgiveness is for me and not them. They have been and are living there lives regardless of what I think say or feel so they have no right to dictate how I choose to forgive.

The last radio interview I done was with Black Treacle talk which is aired on Unity Live Radio it was scary but refreshing and when I listened back to it was devastating and it now made sense as to why I silenced rooms and brought tears to people's eyes when I spoke of my life. I also saw how far I had come and realized that I have always been right to appreciate the little things to get by because those little things that others take for granted have been my big picture. Like the sound of my children's laughter when I'm sat in another room. I worked hard to get my children to that point so I will always appreciate it that little bit more as now they are close out of love and not out of trauma. Completing this book has been another achievement so many times I have sat down to draft this book and have been lucky enough to make it a few pages in as it's just been too much. My biggest achievement to date has been to heal so much that it has fed down to my children who still live with me, and they have begun to heal too and now have a bond that is no longer based on the trauma they were surrounded by but by the fact that they are just brothers who have grown to be close. Now every time I hear them communicate or bellow with laughter it's like a blessing to my ears, a warmth to my heart and a boost to my soul to know I was able to create an environment within their home and within themselves where that could happen.

MY FAMILY TREE

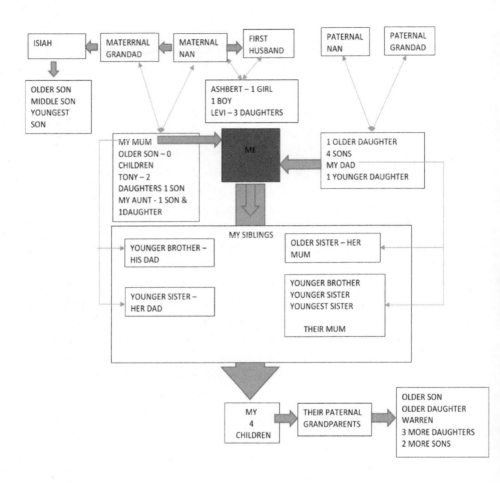

FINISHING NOTES AND THOUGHTS

I have often wondered what my life would have been like without these unfortunate events and what kind of person I would have been. Who I would have had kids with and what they would be like and if I would be a lot further in my life than I am now? There are so many things I wanted to be like an ice skater, a nurse, a midwife, and an air stewardess. Instead, I have been left asking what did I ever do to deserve these things. I know now that I didn't do anything and how could I have done I was only a child when this all started and once a mark had been left it was like it had a left a light on somewhere in my darkness for others to see so they could come and leave their mark too. Even my relationship with my children's father I questioned, maybe it was because I didn't let him be THE man from where I was too independent but then I have to also remind myself that he never showed me that I could rely on him to be the man and do what mattered, what I always did what I could to make things better until there was nothing I could do anymore from where I had grown and he hadn't. Some people believe that it is not down to the woman to teach the man how to be, but you can't expect someone to know how things are if you don't teach them what you like and what you need and how you need to be loved. This works both ways. I think some of my problem was that I didn't have an ideal image I just wanted to be loved so I took what I could get and believed I was worthy of at the time, probably unaware that I was in a world of disassociation at the time. Once the other has been taught only then is there room for excuses.

Everyone who has been in my life has left a scar of some sort and any of those who have passed through have been like a fleet in the night. Not all my scars can be seen but the ones that can be seen and the ones that can't but can by those can see deep enough show moments where I was weak but also show where I was able to survive and are really a sign of the weakness of those who left them.

Those who rape have a lot to answer for as the knock-on effect is huge.

spread your wings, speak your truth, write it down & let it 183 go

Trauma in itself is not easy to deal with but when you are dealing with more traumatic situations than you are built to handle all at one time it's got to be a miracle that anyone comes through the other side and is able to explain why some people do not make it through. I don't know who was first in my ancestral line to be raped but whoever did it is the one who has set this cycle going. Not only for rape but also other forms of abuse but also for the lack of emotional bonds along the ancestral timeline and beyond as well as the lack of being able to trust anyone and not being able to connect to the right people. Which I now hope to be able to do. These things affect us consciously and subconsciously which creates a state of confusion within ourselves which is filtered out onto others, without us always knowing. Some of us are blessed with awareness but even still this can make the task of seeing things difficult. Once you have seen what you need to see you also need to be able to know where to go for help and be ready to be open and honest with yourself as well as with those who are willing to help you. Just noticing isn't enough you need to do more so you can unlearn what is not helpful to you and replace it with what is. You then have to be able to stick to it knowing that at times you will fall back into old behaviour patterns, but the key here is to be able to recognise when that happens, each time you will see this happening earlier and earlier and will be able to do your best to put a stop to old patterns as soon as they happen. No one is perfect but everyone can change if they want to and learn how.

So many things have been closed in terms of being able to find this support which means waiting lists are longer and begs the question what is the point in us the having the support systems when not enough of it is being given? Not just in terms of those who have had to endure trauma but also by the system who sets the consequences. They say innocent until proven guilty yet it's the victims who are left feeling as though they are the ones to blame. When people come to see that rape is not sex but a vicious and violent act of power, it becomes even more so disturbing when it is a child that this is happening to as how sick in the head do you have to be to want to take away innocence from a child, hopefully more will be done. It seems as though it is treated as a sexual act that has gone too far because both of the bodies of the people involved still produce a sexual liquid that you find when having sex. I am not going to call it coming because that is more used in the sense of sexual pleasure and rape is not a pleasurable act especially not for the person who it is happening to. Unfortunately, the genitalia are not aware of this, so it still responds by becoming stimulated, but your mind knows that you don't like what is happening and your flight, fight or freeze response kicks in, hence the confusion.

All trauma needs a space to be worked on and released so the person can heal to have a better life and help to make the world a better place. Instead of going through these things and spending years recovering from the disassociation that is created which is a very emotionally disruptive process, as it involves remembering things that have happened and coping with the things that have happened that you don't even remember alongside the things that you have been a part of without having any emotion to. Ideally, we would want a world with no trauma inflicted by others living in peace with ourselves and each other and only having to deal with whatever mother nature sends our way.

Therapy may not be for everybody, but it is worth it for those that it helps so I believe that instead of reducing the amount of help to others it should have been increased and become more readily available. Whilst I may not be a therapist, even though sometimes I would like to be I would still like to do what I can to help others.

I have also come to realise that some of the anxiety that my children have had has, been some of my mine. Like being scared to let them do things, not seeing things as fair, not liking being left out and not being separated from each other at certain times. I am aware that it's not all stemmed from me as they have grown up in a difficult situation which won't have helped, and their dad has to take some responsibility for who he is and how he is and the actions he has taken and things he has said as well. Through my journey I have seen my blindness in my need to trust only certain people thinking they were doing what was right for me just because they were there.

The system has to take some responsibility to for thinking that children

spread your wings, speak your truth, write it down & let it 185 go

are to blame for what happens to them. Also, things are seen in children so we go directly to them to help them but sometimes it is not them that are broken it is the parents and until the parents can get what they need the child will continue to be the same either forever more or until they come to realise for themselves. By then the only child that needs the help is the inner child of the person.

Also, anxiety isn't always about being stuck in the past having a high level of awareness can also cause you to become anxious as when you can see what is before you and what is either going to come or what is possibly going to come. Those who have anxiety because of the past still need help as no one intentionally sits there thinking about what happens until they become anxious, and we need to remember that it is sitting with what has happened and the thoughts and feelings surrounding it that helps us to process think through and come out the other side and entering the zone of beginning to heal. Being healed can also cause anxiety because you have entered an unknown place and then have to learn to sit with new feelings and thoughts and whilst they will be positive it is not something that you are used to so it seems only normal that you would have anxiety because of this until you have been able to adjust.

More needs to be done for those who are high functioning to as they always seem to either be missed out or last on the list, but they are also more aware hence why they become high functioning. Overworking yourself and pretending to be okay all the time can be just as damaging as someone who locks themselves away. Which is something that high functioning people also do. If you're a parent who is a high functionary this can also add to the emotional disconnect between them and the child. I also believe that it is those who are high functioning who are just as likely if not more likely than someone else to commit suicide in the moment. Them being able to articulate and express themselves should mean that they are heard and not just left to get on with things. Having a high level of insight can make it easier to get the work done and then we may find we have more people around who are equipped to help others in a way that they need to be helped.

On your search for answers, you may find yourself further into darkness and more lost than you were when you started, but at your own pace you just have to keep going and you'll find that you have layers upon layers and as each layer is solved it will give you time to adjust until you're ready to deal with the next one. Then you have to learn to live without the weight of what is holding you down which is really difficult when it's not what you're used to but really worth it. Even if you don't have a family, you still go for it as you are a family to yourself too. You can love you; you can nurture you; you can take you out and you can go out with you and have fun with you.

When you don't have a family even after you have created one if you're blessed enough to you continue to look for a family for you so you can be surrounded by the guidance, connections and love and support that you have longed for to the point of destruction. This is not healthy and sometimes not all it's cracked up to be and can lead you down many blind holes, which just causes you more pain in the long run and hinders your healing. I don't think it's something that ever goes away but it gets easier to live with. I am no longer searching for what I didn't have in others, but I have found it in myself and been able to provide for my kids.

I would like to know love to see it and feel it and know it from another, which I have always wanted but now I know about finding it with the right person and know that real true love is a lot deeper than anything I have ever felt with anyone I have been in a relationship with before, I do believe I have encountered time with my true soul connection but I know he has to be ready to for it to work. I have to be prepared to not run away from it when it comes again no matter scary it feels.

This brings me to love languages we all have one and they vary from person to person, I don't believe that our love languages change we just adjust to how we go about getting it learning not to be accepting of suffering in order to receive it. Sometimes because people do not treat us as we would like to be treated, we believe that they don't love us, but this is not always the case they just aren't aware of how to go about connecting with us in the way we require or simply may not want to.

spread your wings, speak your truth, write it down & let it 187
go

Not everyone knows their own love language so it can be hard for them to articulate what they need let alone be able to cater to you.

I briefly touched upon religion in my story which I am glad that I found it even though I have been doubtful as all members of my family have been brought up around religion, but I had struggled to see any positives within the ones I knew about or had lived around as the dreadful things I had seen them do as individuals under the religion's. I enjoyed learning about Islam and learning how to pray in Arabic, going to the Mendi's and seeing how things were done for the wedding ceremonies. One of the many things it has taught me though is that there is no one person who is more pious than the next. People are still people at the end of the day and will all have our different struggles. So, I now believe that no matter who you are as long as you're living in a good manner that is all anyone can ask.

Mehndi   *Nikah*

Nikah meal settings

Me after I embraced Islam

This time it was different because this journey was personal to me as it was for me, and it gave me a purpose when I needed one and helped me and my children be a family without the need for anyone else. The key thing with it was to follow the religion and not the people which is a good teaching of course as doing what is right should ideally come from within you. It was something that I put every effort into but struggled to maintain and I still found myself coming across the same type of people even those who thought they had changed hadn't they just put the religion in place of their excuse for doing or saying whatever they choose to do. For some it is good as it brings out the good of who they already are and for some it is good as its like it helps them kind of fake it until they make it and some just choose to hide behind it. My biggest struggles were giving up music as that has definitely been the one constant in my life and it became even harder when my fibromyalgia got worse which meant I struggled to keep up with the five washes and prayers throughout the day. So rather than beat myself up about it I have just decided to live as I choose to live and do whatever comes naturally to me. I don't regret my decision and I still choose to cover in a way that I like, I still give to charity and always have done even before finding Islam and do what I can to help others when I can so I can still be there for me to because that is just me and who I have always been no matter what. Now I just don't go out of my way as I used to help others and only do what I can when I can so I can always put my best self forward and I now consider myself to be spiritual rather than religious.

 I still get triggered at different times on different days sometimes for the same reasons and sometimes for varied reasons, but I know that that is my life now and I know how to deal with myself as these things arise and so therefore, I will continue to push forward by continuing to speak my truth and keeping my voice in power.

When I am not writing I like to spend my time meditating or listening to music. Now that I have a clearer head, I also spend some days just sat in silence, which I never used to be able to do. With my newfound self I plan to continue these things whilst also doing more for me with me.

To keep up to date with what I am doing next you can follow me on Instagram where you will also be able to see me and my poetry in action @my_voice_in_power

You can also find me on Facebook, Snapchat and Tik Tok @myvoiceinpower

I also like to craft with Resin, make box frames, create, and print Calendars and T- shirts with my own work. I am still new to starting up a business in this area but to see what I have done so far head on over to www.my.voiceinpower.com

MUCH LOVE TO YOU ALL

.

Printed in Great Britain
by Amazon